ESPIONAGE
And Other Compromises of National Security
Case Summaries from 1975 to 2008

Since its first publication in 1985 as *Recent Espionage Cases,* this product has offered the security educator easy-to-find factual information about espionage-related cases for use in briefings, newsletters, and other educational media. This new edition, issued by the Defense Personnel Security Research Center (PERSEREC), supplements the collection of case summaries with 20 new entries, and updates and expands previous accounts for which we now have more complete information. With this July 2009 edition, we have changed the title to *Espionage and Other Compromises of National Security: Case Summaries from 1975 to 2008* in order to more accurately reflect the range and type of events summarized here.

Purpose: Education and Awareness

The principal objective of this publication is the enhancement of security awareness among cleared employees and military service members by showing that espionage and similar prosecutable offenses involve real people in workplace situations like their own, and that loyal and conscientious employees continue to be the target of attempts by agents of foreign intelligence services to recruit them as sources of sensitive defense and intelligence information. The reader will recognize that these case summaries bear little resemblance to the glamorized fictional accounts of spy novels; rather, they often tell mundane tales of human folly resulting in tragic personal consequences.

Many of the disasters described in these summaries might have been avoided if concerned coworkers, recognizing danger signs and personal vulnerabilities, had been willing to intervene. Other lessons that can be shared with employee audiences are that most offenders were trusted insiders, not foreign agents; even "friendly" countries have been the recipients of stolen US classified information; and these damaging betrayals can occur in either government or contractor organizations.

In addition to serving the needs of the security educator, this publication through several editions since 1985 has been consistently in high demand as a reference source for security managers and policymakers and used in the training of counterintelligence and security professionals in government and industry. We hope that this latest release, *Espionage and Other Compromises of National Security*, will continue to meet these various needs.

Rationale for Including Cases

The principal criterion for including an espionage case summary in this volume is that it involves the theft or compromise, or threat of compromise, of US national defense information. Normally this is interpreted as US classified information, but as a legal concept this may include controlled or critical technologies that have defense application. Every effort has been made to include at least every case, reported in the public media and in open-source government publications, in which a US citizen has been indicted or charged with espionage under the espionage code (generally, several sections of USC Title 18). However, there are a number of cases in this collection that have not been prosecuted under the espionage code. In these events, an insider or private sector business figure, under suspicion of espionage, was tried and often convicted of a lesser offense such as illegal export of militarily critical technology or for the unauthorized removal of classified documents to an unsecure location. These borderline cases should be discussed with cleared employees by security educators since they stand as examples of what can go wrong when sound personnel security policies and practices are not followed.

While our major concern, and by far the cause of the greater number of cases, is insider betrayal, a few summaries included here result from the apprehension of foreign operatives. These agents of adversarial intelligence services have targeted US information or assets or have attempted to enlist the cooperation of a US citizen having legitimate access to classified information. Foreign agent cases are important for their educational value since they highlight the targeting of potentially vulnerable insiders and confirm the persistence of foreign services to infiltrate US government organizations and to recruit cleared employees for illegal activities. Admittedly, many foreign agent operations go unreported in the press. Many agents having diplomatic immunity have been sent home as *personae non gratae* ("PNGed") "for engaging in activities incompatible with their diplomatic status." To assist the security educator in identifying foreign agent cases, we have marked these with an asterisk in each listing.

The year 1975 was selected as the starting point for these case summaries as it marked the end of a 10-year period of relative quiet in the active prosecution of espionage cases. According to news reports, the government decided to resume aggressive prosecution of arrested spies in the mid-1970s. Within each year of the decade that followed, the number of cases brought to court had risen to nearly a dozen. The high frequency of prosecutions in the 1980s and 1990s argued for changing the title of this publication since these cases, however instructive, are no longer recent. The collection now includes 141 case summaries in which US information or assets have been targeted. New cases will be added in future updates. We have also attempted to provide assistance to the user by including three listings of cases in the introduction: (1) alphabetical by name of offender, (2) chronological by date of arrest or first public disclosure, and (3) by targeted or affected organization. Thus, the security educator can find a particular summary by referencing the name of the culprit, the most recent case events, or those cases involving a particular targeted organization.

Each case summary identifies one or more offenders who were implicated in an effort to illegally provide US classified or other sensitive national defense information to a foreign interest or in an activity that seriously compromised national security information. Each summary is identified by the name of a person who was officially named or indicted on at least one count of espionage or espionage-related offenses. The authors offer selected citations at the end of case summaries should a reader wish to refer to original sources for more information.

Further Analysis of Espionage Data

Espionage and Other Compromises of National Security is closely related to PERSEREC's long-standing study of espionage as one manifestation of betrayal of trust among members of the government and contractor workforce. Espionage is a rare crime; however, it is one that when undetected can have devastating consequences for national security. Security educators, who might be interested in a more detailed overview of espionage as a phenomenon in terms of frequency distributions on several key variables, can find this in a PERSEREC technical report, *Changes in Espionage by Americans, 1947-2007.* This and earlier reports on espionage trends can also be found on the PERSEREC website under Selected Reports. The 2007 report on espionage changes shows the number of espionage offenders who fall into various categories such as personal attributes, motivation, modus operandi, and consequences for the offender.

Table of Contents

Case Summaries by Name of Principal Offender

Case Summaries by Year of Arrest or First Public Disclosure of Involvement in Espionage

1975   Dedeyan, Sadag K.

1976   Moore, Edwin G., II

1977   Boyce, Christopher John
        Rogalsky, Ivan N.*

1978   Enger, Valdik*
        Humphrey, Ronald
        Kampiles, William

1979   Madsen, Lee Eugene

1980   Barnett, David Henry
        Herrmann, Rudolph Albert*

1981   Baba, Stephen Anthony
        Bell, William Holden
        Cooke, Christopher Michael
        Helmich, Joseph George
        Murphy, Michael Richard

1982   Gilbert, Otto Attila*
        Horton, Brian Patrick
        Slavens, Brian Everett

1983   Dubberstein, Waldo H.
        Ellis, Robert Wade
        Harper, James Durward
        Kostadinov, Penyu B.*
        Leonov, Yuriy P.*
        Maynard, John Raymond
        Mira, Francisco de Assis
        Pickering, Jeffery Loring
        Wold, Hans Palmer
        Zehe, Alfred*

1984   Cavanagh, Thomas Patrick
        Cordrey, Robert Ernest
        Forbrich, Ernst*
        Kearn, Bruce Leland
        Koecher, Karl Frantisek*
        Michelson, Alice*
        Miller, Richard W.
        Morison, Samuel Loring
        Slatten, Charles Dale
        Smith, Richard Craig
        Wolff, Jay Clyde

1985   Buchanan, Edward Owen
        Chin, Larry Wu-Tai*
        Hawkins, Stephen Dwayne

        Howard, Edward Lee
        Jeffries, Randy Miles
        Pelton, Ronald William
        Pollard, Jonathan Jay
        Scranage, Sharon Marie
        Tobias, Michael Timothy
        Walker, Arthur James
        Walker, John Anthony
        Whitworth, Jerry Alfred

1986   Allen, Michael Hahn
        Davies, Allen John
        Haguewood, Robert Dean
        Ismaylov, Vladimir M.*
        Lonetree, Clayton John
        Ott, Bruce Damian
        Zakharov, Gennadiy F.*

1987   Tumanova, Svetlana

1988   Conrad, Clyde Lee
        Desheng, Hou*
        Dolce, Thomas Joseph
        Fleming, David
        Garcia, Wilfredo
        Hall, James III
        Ratkai, Stephen Joseph*
        Richardson, Daniel Walter
        Souther, Glenn Michael
        Spade, Henry Otto
        Tsou, Douglas

1989   King, Donald Wayne
        Kunkle, Craig Dee
        Mortati, Tommaso
        Nesbitt, Frank Arnold
        Pakhtusov, Yuri N.*
        Peri, Michael A.
        Schoof, Charles Edward
        Wilmoth, James R.
        Wolf, Ronald Craig

1990   Hoffman, Ronald
        Ramsay, Roderick James

1991   Anzalone, Charles Lee Francis
        Carney, Jeffrey M.
        Sombolay, Albert T.

1992   Brown, Joseph Garfield
        Rondeau, Jeffrey Stephen

1993   Gregory, Jeffery Eugene

Hamilton, Frederick Christopher
Jones, Geneva
Kao, Yen Men*
Lalas, Steven John

1994   Ames, Aldrich Hazen

1995   Charlton, John Douglas
Kota, Subrahmanyam
Schwartz, Michael Stephen

1996   Jenott, Eric O.
Kim, Robert Chaegun
Lessenthien, Kurt G.
Lipka, Robert Stephan
Nicholson, Harold James
Pitts, Earl Edwin
Seldon, Phillip Tyler

1997   Clark, James Michael
Lee, Peter H.
Stand, Kurt Alan
Warren, Kelly Therese

1998   Alonso, Alejandro
Boone, David Sheldon
Groat, Douglas Frederick
Guerrero, Antonio (see also Hernandez, Gerardo)
Hernandez, Gerardo*
Hernandez, Linda*
Santos, Joseph

1999   Wispelaere, Jean-Philippe

2000   Faget, Mariano
Smith, Timothy Steven
Trofimoff, George

2001   Hanssen, Robert Philip
Montes, Ana Belen
Regan, Brian Patrick

2003   Mehalba, Ahmed Fathy
Smith, James J.
Yai, John Joungwoong

2004   Anderson, Ryan Gibson
Ford, Kenneth Wayne, Jr.
Keyser, Donald Willis
Montaperto, Ronald N.

2005   Aragoncillo, Leandro
Franklin, Lawrence Anthony
Mak, Chi
Nour, Almaliki
Shaaban, Hafiz Ahmed Ali Shaaban*

2006   Diaz, Matthew M.
Maziarz, Gary
Weinmann, Ariel Jonathan

2007   Abu-Jihaad, Hassan
Oakley, Roy L.

2008   Kadish, Ben-Ami
Kuo, Tai Shen*
Roth, John Reece
Shu, Quan-Sheng

Espionage Case Summaries by Targeted or Victimized Organization
(In some cases a specific US target organization cannot be identified)

Army 1981-1989

Conrad, Clyde Lee	10
Dolce, Thomas Joseph	13
Forbrich, Ernst*	15
Gilbert, Otto Attila*	16
Hall, James III	18
Helmich, Joseph George	21
Michelson, Alice*	37
Mortati, Tommaso	40
Peri, Michael A.	44
Richardson, Daniel Walter	48
Slatten, Charles Dale	52
Smith, Richard Craig	54
Tumanova, Svetlana	58

Army 1990-2008

Anderson, Ryan Gibson	3
Boone, David Sheldon	5
Clark, James M.	9
Gregory, Jeffery Eugene	17
Jenott, Eric O.	25
Kadish, Ben-Ami	26
Lalas, Steven John	32
Lipka, Robert Stephan	34
Nour, Almaliki	42
Ramsay, Roderick James	46
Rondeau, Jeffrey S.	48
Seldon, Phillip Tyler	51
Sombolay, Albert T.	55
Trofimoff, George	57
Warren, Kelly Therese	59

Navy 1978-1984

Baba, Stephen Anthony	4
Ellis, Robert Wade	13
Enger, Valdik*	13
Horton, Brian Patrick	23
Kearn, Bruce Leland	28
Madsen, Lee Eugene	35
Maynard, John Raymond	36
Morison, Samuel Loring	40
Murphy, Michael Richard	41
Pickering, Jeffery	44
Wold, Hans Palmer	61
Wolff, Jay Clyde	62
Zehe, Alfred*	63

Navy 1985-1988

Allen, Michael Hahn	1
Fleming, David	14
Garcia, Wilfredo	16
Haguewood, Robert Dean	18
Hawkins, Stephen Dwayne	20
Pollard, Jonathan Jay	45
Ratkai, Stephen Joseph*	47
Souther, Glenn Michael	55
Spade, Henry Otto	56
Tobias, Michael Timothy	56
Walker, Arthur James	58
Walker, John Anthony	58
Whitworth, Jerry Alfred	60

Navy 1989-2008

Diaz, Matthew M.	12
Guerrero, Antonio	18
Kao, Yen Men*	27
Kim, Robert Chaegun	28
King, Donald Wayne	29
Kunkle, Craig Dee	31
Lessenthien, Kurt G.	33
Schoof, Charles Edward	50
Schwartz, Michael Stephen	50
Smith, Timothy Steven	54
Wilmoth, James R.	61
Weinmann, Ariel Jonathan	60

Marine Corps

Anzalone, Charles Lee Francis	3
Cordrey, Robert Ernest	11
Lonetree, Clayton John	34
Maziarz, Gary	36
Nesbitt, Frank Arnold	41
Slavens, Brian Everett	53

Air Force

Buchanan, Edward Owen	7
Carney, Jeffrey M.	7
Cooke, Christopher Michael	11
Davies, Allen John	11
Ismaylov, Vladimir M.*	24
Mira, Francisco de Assis	38
Nesbitt, Frank Arnold	41
Ott, Bruce Damian	43
Roth, John Reece	49
Wolf, Ronald Craig	62

ABU-JIHAAD, HASSAN (formerly Paul R. Hall), a Navy signalman honorably discharged in 2002, was arrested on 27 March 2007, in Phoenix, Arizona, charged with providing classified information on ship movements to al-Qaida operatives in London. These operatives maintained a network of websites believed to be a conduit for money and weapons to al-Qaida. A search of the network operator's apartment by British law enforcement officers in December 2003 revealed a floppy disk with an email reportedly containing information about ship movements, armaments, vulnerabilities and the formation of a US naval battle group allegedly provided by the ex-seaman. As a signalman aboard the USS *Benfold*, Abu-Jihaad held a Secret security clearance and had access to all compromised information. He was accused of having informed his al-Qaida contact that the *Benfold* would be particularly vulnerable to rocket-propelled grenades from a small ship as it passed through the Strait of Hormuz. He pleaded not guilty to all charges of espionage. At his trial the presiding judge advised jurors that whoever provided the compromised information to al-Qaida did so with the intent to kill US citizens. Sentencing, originally set for May 2008, was delayed as defense attorneys petitioned the court for a new trial on the grounds that the evidence did not conclusively link their client with the compromised information. Abu-Jihaad was convicted of espionage on 6 March 2008. He had converted to Islam and changed his name in 1997. Eight months later he enlisted in the Navy. Following his discharge, he worked for the United Parcel Service. In March 2009, a federal judge dismissed his conviction for providing support to terrorists, but upheld his conviction for disclosing classified information. On 3 April 2009 Abu-Jihaad was sentenced to 10 years in prison.

The Courant, New Haven, CT   26 Feb 2008, "Sailor's Terror Trial Opens with Story of Discovery"
The Advocate, Stamford, CT   28 Feb 2008, "Prosecutors Try to Show Leaked Documents Matched Ship
                                      Movements"
New York Times   29 Feb 2008, "Prosecutors Rest in Navy Terrorism Case"
Department of Justice,   6 Mar 2008, "Jury Finds Former Member of U.S. Navy Guilty of Terrorism and
     Press Release   Espionage Charges"

ALLEN, MICHAEL HAHN, a retired Navy Senior Chief Radioman employed at the Cubi Point Naval Air Station in the Philippines, was arrested on suspicion of espionage by Navy security agents on 4 December 1986. Allen, who had been working as a civilian clerk, retired from the Navy in 1972. The employee confessed to passing classified US counterintelligence reports to Philippine intelligence officers after seeing a videotape of himself hiding documents in his pockets. When apprehended he had a photocopy of a Secret page on his person; six other classified documents were seized at his residence. The charges covered the period between July and December 1986 during which time he was accused of photocopying and removing classified material from the communication center. According to the Naval Investigative Service, Allen's activities may have resulted in the compromising of important Filipino intelligence sources. Prosecutors argued that Allen's main reason for providing secrets to the Filipinos was to promote his local business interests that included a used car dealership, a bar, and a cockfighting ring. On 14 August 1987, a court martial in San Diego found Allen guilty of 10 counts of espionage and sentenced him to eight years in prison. The six-officer panel also imposed a $10,000 fine on the former radioman.

New York Times   12 Dec 1986, "Navy Employee Held in Espionage-Related Case"
Los Angeles Times   15 Aug 1987, "Linked to Filipinos; Ex-Navy Man Found Guilty "

ALONSO, ALEJANDRO, 39, a member of the "La Red Avispa" (the Red Wasp Network), a Cuban spy ring in south Florida, was arrested with nine other members of the ring on 12 September 12 1998 and charged with conspiracy to commit espionage. [See also Linda Hernandez, Gerardo Hernandez and Joseph Santos.] Alonso was born in Des Moines, Iowa, but returned to Cuba and was recruited there by the Cuban Intelligence Service. In 1994 he began trying to collect information on military installations in south Florida and on the activities of the Cuban-American exile community there. Alonso, a boat pilot, joined an exile group called the Democracy Movement to report on their plans from the inside, and he participated in boat flotillas held to protest Cuba's Communist government. He pleaded guilty in a plea bargain to being an unregistered agent of a foreign government, and was sentenced on 28 January 2000 in US District Court in Miami to seven years in prison.

Associated Press   19 Sep 1998, "Bail Denied for Accused Cuban Spy"
Miami Herald   29 Jan 2000, "Confessed Cuban Spy Receives Seven Years"

AMES, ALDRICH HAZEN, CIA intelligence officer and his Colombian-born wife **MARIA DEL ROSARIO CASAS AMES**, were arrested 21 February 1994, after various attempts since 1985 to identify a mole in the CIA. The arrests followed a 10-month investigation that focused on Rick Ames. He was charged with providing highly classified information to the Soviet KGB and later, to its successor, the Russian SVR, over a nine-year period. From 1983 to 1985, Ames had been assigned to the counterintelligence unit in the agency's Soviet/East European Division, where he was responsible for directing the analysis of Soviet intelligence operations. In this capacity he would have known about any penetration of the Soviet military or the KGB. According to press reports, the trail that led to the arrest of Ames and his wife began in 1987 after the unexplained disappearance or deaths of numerous US intelligence sources overseas. According to court documents, Ames' information allowed the Russians to close down at least 100 intelligence operations and led to the execution of the agents in Russia that he betrayed. Despite reports of alcohol abuse, sexual misconduct, and repeated security violations, Ames was promoted into positions at the CIA that allowed him to steal increasingly sensitive information while he was spying for the Soviets. Facing alimony payments and the financial demands of his new wife, Rosario, in April 1985 Ames decided to get money by volunteering to spy for the Russians. He first contacted the KGB by dropping a note at the Soviet Embassy. Over his nine years of espionage activity, he removed bags of documents from CIA facilities, without challenge, and deposited them at dead drops around Washington or met his handlers at meetings around the world. Ames reportedly received up to $2.5 million from the Russians over this period of time. Reports of the couple's high-rolling life style included the cash purchase of a half-million dollar home, credit card bills of $455,000, and a new Jaguar sports car. But despite his unexplained affluence, Ames' story that his wife had wealthy relatives in Colombia satisfied doubts about his income for years, until a CIA counterintelligence investigator finally checked the cover story with sources in Colombia. A search of Ames' office uncovered 144 classified intelligence reports not related to his current assignment in CIA's Counternarcotics Center. The Director of Central Intelligence reported to Congress that Ames' espionage caused "severe, wide-ranging, and continuing damage to US national security interests," making Ames one of the most damaging spies in US history. He provided the Soviets, and later the Russians, with the identities of 10 US clandestine agents (at least nine of whom were executed), the identities of many US agents run against the Russians, methods of double agent operations and communications, details on US counterintelligence operations, identities of CIA and other intelligence personnel, technical collection activities, analytic techniques, and intelligence reports, arms control papers, and the cable traffic of several federal departments. On 28 April 1994, Aldrich Ames and his wife pleaded guilty to conspiring to commit espionage and to evading taxes. Ames was immediately sentenced to life imprisonment without parole. Under the plea agreement, Maria Rosario Ames was sentenced to five years and three months in prison for conspiring to commit espionage and evading taxes on $2.5 million obtained by her husband for his illegal activities.

New York Times   22 Feb 1994, "Ex-Branch Leader of C.I.A. is Charged as a Russian Agent"
Washington Post   23 Feb 1994, "CIA Officer Charged With Selling Secrets"
Washington Post   25 Feb 1994, "Accused Couple Came From Different Worlds"
U.S. Senate Select Committee   1 Nov 1994, "An Assessment of the Aldrich H. Ames Espionage Case and
   on Intelligence   Its Implications for U.S. Intelligence"

Washington Post	27 Dec 1994, "Ames Says CIA Does Not Believe He Has Told All"
Washington Post	11 Jun 1995, "The Man Who Sold the Secrets"
Los Angeles Times	22 Oct 1994, "Wife of CIA Double Agent Sentenced to 5 Years in Prison"

ANDERSON, RYAN GIBSON, 26, a Specialist and tank crewman in the Washington National Guard, was arrested on February 12, 2004, and charged with five counts of attempting to provide aid and information to the enemy, Al Qaeda. Anderson converted from his Lutheran upbringing to Islam in college while attending Washington State University, where he studied Middle Eastern military history and graduated with a B.A. in 2002. In late 2003, as his National Guard unit was preparing to deploy to the war in Iraq, Anderson went onto Internet chat rooms and sent emails trying to make contact with Al Qaeda cells in the U.S. His emails were noticed by an amateur anti-terrorist Internet monitor, Shannen Rossmiller, a city judge in Montana who had begun monitoring Islamist Jihad websites in an effort to contribute to homeland defense after the 9/11 attacks. After she identified him by tracing his Arab pseudonym, Amir Abdul Rashid, Rossmiller passed along to the FBI her suspicions about Anderson. In a joint DOJ and FBI sting operation conducted in late January 2004, Anderson was videotaped offering to persons he thought were Al Qaeda operatives, sketches of M1A1 and M1A2 tanks, a computer disk with his identifying information and photo, and information about Army weapons systems, including "the exact caliber of round needed to penetrate the windshield and kill the driver of an up-armored Humvee." At his Army court martial the defense argued that Anderson suffered from various mental conditions including bipolar disorder and a high-performing type of autism, which led to role playing, exaggeration of his abilities, and repeated attempts to gain social acceptance. The prosecution argued that what he did constituted treason. The court-martial convicted Anderson on all five counts and on 3 September, 2004, and sentenced him to life in prison with possibility of parole, demotion to the rank of private, and a dishonorable discharge.

New York Times	13 Feb 2004, "Guardsman Taken Into Custody and Examine or Qaeda Tie"
New York Post	12 Jul 2004, "Lady Who 'Nets Spies'"
Seattle Times	31 Aug 2004, "Guardsman Anderson Accused of 'Betrayal' as Court Martial Begins"
Seattle Post-Intelligencer	2 Sep 2004, "Accused GI Called Bipolar, 'Social Misfit'"
New York Times	4 Sep 2004, "Guardsman Given Life in Prison for Trying to Help Al Qaeda"

ANZALONE, CHARLES LEE FRANCIS, a 23-year old Marine corporal stationed in Yuma, Arizona, was arrested 13 February 1991 after a four-month investigation and charged with suspicion of attempted espionage. In November 1990, Anzalone, a telephone lineman, called the Soviet Embassy in Washington to offer his services as a spy (under the pretext of asking about a college scholarship). An FBI agent posing as a KGB intelligence officer contacted Anzalone who passed him two technical manuals about cryptographic equipment, a security badge, and guard schedules. Anzalone, who is part Mohawk, told the agent that he hated capitalism, the American government, and held a grudge against the nation's treatment of native Americans. Anzalone testified that his offering to spy was a ruse to get money from the Soviets. On 3 May 1991, Anzalone was found guilty of attempted espionage. He was also convicted of adultery with the wife of another Marine stationed in the Persian Gulf, and of possession and use of marijuana. He was sentenced to 15 years in prison.

| *San Diego Union* | 2 May 1991, "Tape Shows Marine and Soviet Spy" |
| *Los Angeles Times* | 4 May 1991, "Marine Guilty in Spying Case" |

ARAGONCILLO, LEANDRO, a naturalized US citizen of Filipino origin, was arrested on 10 September 2005, charged with passing classified intelligence reports regarding the Philippines to current and former officials of that country during a period when he worked at the White House and, later, in 2005, from his FBI office. The material was passed to **MICHAEL RAY AQUINO**, a former deputy director of the Philippines National Police and a Philippine national who was then living in New York. Aragoncillo passed documents to Aquino by way of cell phone text messages, email and CDs. The documents then were transferred to opposition politicians in the Philippines. Aragoncillo came to the US in 1982, and joined the Marine Corps in 1983, retiring in 2004 as a sergeant. He had been assigned (1999-2002) to the White House as staff assistant to military advisors in the Office of the Vice President, serving under Vice Presidents Gore and Cheney. President Clinton introduced Aragoncillo to Philippine president, Joseph Estrada, at the White House during Estrada's official state visit to the US in 2000. Aragoncillo handed Estrada his card. Later he was approached by an Estrada associate and asked to pass along American intelligence that could be used to save Estrada's presidency. (Estrada was eventually removed from office through impeachment in 2001.) Thus, while working for Cheney, Aragoncillo began stealing information about Filipino politicians and American policy towards the Philippines. He would walk out of the White House on a fairly regular basis with disks of classified documents in his bag and even use the White House fax to send documents directly to the Philippines. When his White House assignment ended in 2002, Aragoncillo sought positions in other parts of government, eventually in 2004 landing a job as an intelligence analyst at the FBI's Information Technology Center. From there he resumed sending classified documents via his courier, Aquino, to Filipino opposition politicians, who were trying to overthrow Estrada's successor, President Gloria Arroyo. The FBI's investigation began after Aragoncillo intervened with US immigration officials on behalf of Aquino, who was facing deportation for overstaying his visa. Suspicious officials notified the FBI, who began an audit of Aragoncillo's computer activities at his FBI office. They discovered that he had been making unauthorized queries of FBI databases and printing or downloading classified documents related to the Philippines. Aragoncillo was sentenced on 16 July 2007 to 10 years in prison, Aquino to six years and four months. In February 2009 it was determined that Aquino's sentence was based on a mistaken interpretation of federal guidelines and that his new sentence would range from 36 to 46 months, to include time already served since September 2005.

cicentre.com	n.d., "Espionage/Spy Case: Leandro Aragoncillo and Michael Ray Aquino"
FoxNews.com	12 Sep 2005, "FBI Analyst, Filipino Charged With Spying"
New York Times	13 Sep 2005, "Two Men are Charged with Passing Secrets to Philippines"
Reuters	18 Jul 2007, "Ex-Cheney Aide Gets 10 Years in Prison in Spy Case"
Newsday.com	6 Feb 2009, "Court Vacates Sentence of Filipino in Spy Case"

BABA, STEPHEN ANTHONY, an ensign in the US Navy, was arrested on 1 October 1981 for sending a classified electronic warfare document and two microfilm indices of key code words to the South African Embassy in Washington, DC. He reportedly asked for an initial payment of $50,000 for the material. Other charges against Baba at the time included armed robbery, extortion, and assault. Baba mailed the documents from his frigate, the USS *Lang*, in September 1981, while stationed at San Diego. The South African Embassy returned the unsolicited materials to US officials. In court testimony it was asserted that Baba had attempted to sell documents to raise money for his fiancée in the Philippines so that she could attend college. He pleaded guilty and was sentenced 20 January 1982 by court-martial to eight years of hard labor.

New York Times	4 Dec 1981, "Ensign is Accused in Navy Spy Case"
Washington Post	21 Jan 1982, "Ensign Sentenced to Hard Labor for Sending Data to S. Africa"

BARNETT, DAVID HENRY, a CIA officer, was indicted 24 October 1980 for having sold to the Soviet Union details of one of the CIA's most successful undercover operations, code-named "Habrink." Following a tour of duty in Indonesia between 1967 and 1970, Barnett resigned from the CIA to enter private business. In late 1976, faced with failure and debts of $100,000, he offered to sell classified information to the KGB. Barnett handed over full details of Habrink to the KGB, including CIA information on the Soviet SA-2 surface-to-air missile and the Whiskey class diesel-powered submarine. He also revealed the names of 30 CIA intelligence officers as well as the identities of informants recruited by the CIA. In all, Barnett was paid approximately $92,000 by the KGB for information supplied between 1976 and 1977. US agents reportedly spotted Barnett meeting the KGB in Vienna in April 1980; he was questioned by the FBI upon his return to the US. Barnett entered a plea of guilty and received an 18-year sentence. He was paroled in 1990.

New York Times	23 Oct 1980, "Alleged Spy Sought 2nd Post, Aides Say"
New York Times	30 Oct 1980, "Ex-Agent of C.I.A. Pleads Guilty"
Washington Post	30 Oct 1980, "Ex-CIA Agent Pleads Guilty to Spying"

BELL, WILLIAM HOLDEN, project manager of the Radar Systems Group at Hughes Aircraft in El Segundo, California, and **MARIAN ZACHARSKI**, president of the Polish American Machinery Corporation (POLAMCO), were arraigned in June 1981 on espionage charges. Bell had been faced with financial difficulties; Zacharski in reality was an officer of the Polish intelligence service. Under the guise of business activities, and over a period of several months, Zacharski developed a relationship with Bell that resulted in the transfer of Secret documents for more than $150,000. As a result, the "quiet radar" and other sophisticated systems developed at Hughes Aircraft were seriously compromised. On 24 June, Bell was confronted by FBI agents with the fact of his involvement in espionage that had been independently established. He confessed and agreed to cooperate with the FBI in the effort to apprehend Zacharski. On 14 December, Zacharski was convicted of espionage and received a life sentence. Bell, who pleaded guilty, was sentenced to eight years. In June 1985 Zacharski was exchanged, along with three other Soviet Bloc spies, for 25 persons held in Eastern Europe. This case is seen as a classic example of recruitment of cleared US personnel for espionage by hostile intelligence operatives.

Chicago Tribune	20 May 1984, "Real-life Spy Tale Robbed of an Ending"
DoD Security Institute, *Security Awareness Bulletin*	No. 3-83, June 1983, "Caught Unawares: The Case of William Bell and Marian Zacharski"
John Barron, *KGB Today: The Hidden Hand*, 1983	

BOONE, DAVID SHELDON, a former Army signals analyst for the National Security Agency, was arrested 10 October 1998, and charged with selling Top Secret documents to agents of the Soviet Union from 1988 to 1991. Compromised documents including a 600-page manual describing US reconnaissance programs and a listing of nuclear targets in Russia. Boone was arrested at a suburban Virginia hotel after being lured from his home in Germany to the United States in a FBI sting operation. He had worked for NSA for three years before being reassigned to Augsburg, Germany, in 1988, and retired from the Army in 1991. In October 1988, the same month that he separated from his wife and children, Boone walked into the Soviet Embassy in Washington and offered his services. According to an FBI counterintelligence agent's affidavit, Boone was under "severe financial and personal difficulties" when he began spying. His former wife had garnished his Army sergeant's pay, leaving him with only $250 a month. According to the Federal complaint, Boone met with his handler about four times a year from late 1988 until June 1990, when his access to classified information was suspended because of "his lack of personal and professional responsibility." He held a Top Secret clearance from 1971 and gained access to SCI information in 1976. He is alleged to have received payments totaling more than $60,000 from the KGB.

Boone was indicted on three counts: one for conspiracy to commit espionage and the other two related to his alleged passing of two Top Secret documents to his Soviet handler. On 18 December, Boon pleaded guilty to conspiracy, and on 26 February 1999 he was sentenced to 24 years and four months in prison. Under a plea agreement Boone was also required to forfeit $52,000 and a hand-held scanner he used to copy documents.

Washington Post	6 Nov 1998, "Ex-NSA Indicted for Spying"
Washington Post	9 Nov 1998, "Trial Set for Ex-NSA Analyst"
Washington Post	27 Feb 1999, "Ex-NSA Worker Gets 24 Years for Spying"

BOYCE, CHRISTOPHER JOHN, an employee of TRW Inc., a California-based defense contractor, and his friend, **ANDREW DAULTON LEE**, were arrested in January 1977 for selling classified information to the Soviets. Over a period of several months, Boyce, employed as a code clerk in a heavily guarded communications center at TRW, removed classified code material and passed it along to Lee who in turn delivered it to KGB agents in Mexico City. Boyce, son of a former FBI agent, and his childhood friend Lee had grown up in affluent Palos Verde, in southern California. Both were altar boys together and later played on the high school football team. Boyce claimed to have discovered while working in the vault that the US government was spying not only on the country's enemies but also on an ally, Australia. He decided to strike back by hatching a plan to sabotage the US intelligence network. He recruited Lee to help him sell classified information to the Russians. Boyce was probably motivated also by youthful rebelliousness and perhaps a craving for danger and excitement. This was likely accompanied by the need for money with which he and Lee could purchase drugs, a taste developed during their teenage years. The espionage activity, which netted the pair $70,000, was discovered only after Lee's arrest by Mexican police as he attempted to deliver yet another set of classified material at the Soviet Embassy in Mexico City. Film strips marked Top Secret found on Lee by Mexican authorities were turned over to American officials. Under questioning by Mexican security police and FBI representatives, Lee implicated Boyce, who was arrested on 16 January in California. The pair were reported to have seriously compromised the Ryolite surveillance satellite system developed at TRW. Lee was sentenced to life in prison, Boyce to 40 years. In 1980 Boyce escaped and spent 19 months as a fugitive. Following Boyce's second apprehension, his sentence was increased by 28 years. He was finally released from prison in March 2003 at the age of 50.

New York Times	13 Apr 1977, "Alleged Spy for Soviets Linked to C.I.A"
New York Times	27 Apr 1977, "Man Said to Admit Spying for Soviets"
New York Times	22 May 1977, "To Be Young, Rich—and a Spy"
Lindsey, Robert, *The Falcon and the Snowman*, 1979	
Testimony of Christopher J. Boyce before the Permanent Subcommittee on Investigations, April 1985	

BROWN, JOSEPH GARFIELD, former US airman and martial arts instructor, was arrested by FBI agents on 27 December 1992, and charged with spying for the Philippine government. Brown allegedly provided an official there with illegally obtained secret CIA documents on Iraqi terrorist activities during the Persian Gulf War and assassination plans by a Philippine insurgent group. The former US airman was arrested at Dulles International Airport after being lured to the US from the Philippines by undercover FBI agents with the promise of a job teaching self-defense tactics to CIA agents. On the following day he was indicted on three counts of espionage in Federal court in Alexandria, Virginia. Brown enlisted in the US Air Force in 1966 and served until 1968. He continued to reside in the Philippines, working as a martial arts instructor for the Department of Tourism until the time of his arrest. He is accused of obtaining classified documents in 1990 and 1991 in Manila from CIA secretary, **VIRGINIA JEAN BAYNES**, and passing them to a Philippine government official. An FBI spokesman stated that Baynes pleaded guilty to espionage in Federal court on 22 May 1992, and served a 41-month prison term. The FBI began its investigation in April 1991 after an internal CIA inquiry determined that Baynes, who joined the agency in 1987 and who was assigned two years later to the embassy in Manila, had passed two or three classified documents to Brown. Baynes had met Brown when she enrolled in a karate class which he taught at an embassy annex. According to Baynes, as the friendship between her and Brown grew in the late summer of 1990, he asked her to obtain CIA information on assassinations planned by an insurgent group that were to be carried out in the Philippines. In a wish to please Brown, Baynes, who held a Top Secret clearance, complied with his request by removing secret documents from the embassy. Brown, motivated by the hope of acquiring money for his espionage, pleaded guilty in April 1993 to a charge of conspiring to commit espionage by delivering secret CIA documents to a Philippine government official. He was sentenced to nearly six years in prison.

Los Angeles Times   29 Dec 1992, "Ex-US Airman Charged With Espionage"
Washington Post   6 Jan 1993, "Spy Charge Played Down by Official"

BUCHANAN, EDWARD OWEN. In early May 1985, an Air Force Office of Special Investigations (AFOSI) human source provided information that Airman Edward O. Buchanan, in training at Lowry AFB, Colorado, had been phoning the East German Embassy in Washington, DC. He reportedly wanted to know if embassy officials had received a letter he had sent in April 1985. According to the source, the letter contained an offer by Buchanan to commit espionage for the East German Government. Unsuccessful at making an East German contact, Buchanan then mailed a letter to the Soviet Embassy in Washington, DC, fully identifying himself and stating that he had information of a scientific and technological nature that he wanted to sell to the Russian government. He indicated he would continue to conduct business with the Soviets if they liked his material. At this point AFOSI agents, posing as Soviet representatives, contacted Buchanan. Believing that he was doing business with Soviet intelligence officers, the Airman offered to commit espionage and sell classified documents. He then provided documents to the undercover AFOSI/FBI agents that he claimed were classified Secret and was paid $1,000. Buchanan was apprehended immediately. A later examination of the documents disclosed that they were copies of unclassified articles from an electronics magazine. During an interview following his arrest, Buchanan admitted contacting the East German Embassy and the Soviet Embassy for the purpose of committing espionage. Buchanan also admitted that, although he did not have access to classified information at that time (because of his student status), he planned to sell classified information once his clearance had been granted and he was assigned to a base in Germany. At the time he was being processed for a Top Secret - Special Compartmented Information clearance. His stated intention was to establish a business relationship with the Soviets by selling bogus material to "get my foot in the door" and then later sell classified information. He would then "sell as much classified material as he could until he made enough money to live comfortably." Buchanan was court-martialed on 26 August 1985, and sentenced to 30 months' confinement, reduction to Airman Basic, forfeiture of all pay and allowances, and a dishonorable discharge.

CARNEY, JEFFREY M., former intelligence specialist with the Air Force, was apprehended in 1991 in East Berlin on charges of espionage after the fall of the Berlin Wall. Carney entered the Air Force in December 1980. From April 1982 to April 1984 he was stationed at Tempelhof Central Airport in Berlin where he was a linguist and intelligence specialist. He was assigned to an electronics security group that worked for NSA and eavesdropped on communications of Eastern Bloc countries. While at Tempelhof, he began copying classified documents which he then provided to the East German Ministry for State Security (Stasi) by repeatedly crossing back and forth into East Berlin. In 1984 he was transferred to Goodfellow AFB in Texas where he worked as a language instructor while continuing to spy for East Germany. In 1985, perhaps fearing that he would be caught for his espionage activities, he deserted the

Air Force and defected to East Germany. There he continued to aid the Communist government by intercepting and translating official telephone communications of US military commanders and embassy officials in Berlin. Carney had apparently become disillusioned with the Air Force. He later claimed to have been lonely, alienated, and under psychological stress, and he felt he had no one to talk to about his problems. He had intended to defect to East Germany on his first crossing, but he allowed himself to be drawn into espionage by East German agents who expertly manipulated him and claimed his complete loyalty. The break in the case came after the fall of the Berlin Wall in November 1989, when many Stasi records became available to foreign investigators. In April 1991 he was arrested by Air Force OSI agents at his residence in what used to be in the Soviet sector of Berlin. After being extensively debriefed, Carney pleaded guilty to charges of espionage, conspiracy, and desertion and was sentenced in December 1991 to 38 years in prison. He was released in 2003, after serving 11 years of what eventually became a reduced sentence of 20 years.

Cincinnati Post	21 Dec 1991, "US Spy Gets 38 Years"
Air Force Times	6 Jan 1992, "Ex-Intelligence Specialist Guilty of Spying"
Telegraph (UK)	7 Jul 2003, "Nobody Wants the American Who Gave Secrets to the Stasi"

CAVANAGH, THOMAS PATRICK, an engineering specialist for Northrop Corporation's Advanced Systems Division holding a Secret clearance, was arrested on 18 December 1984 and charged with attempting to sell classified documents on Stealth aircraft technology to the Soviets. It is reported that Cavanagh's attempt to arrange a meeting with a Soviet official by contacting the Soviet Embassy from a pay phone was intercepted. In this call he proposed a meeting in a bar near Los Angeles International Airport where a deal could be negotiated. He was met by FBI undercover agents posing as Soviet representatives. Cavanagh told the agents that the documents and blueprints he had taken from the firm were of highest value to the United States and that "once they were in the hands of the Soviets, they would save them billions." During a subsequent meeting, agents provided the $25,000 demanded for classified documents and made the arrest. Cavanagh, recently separated from his wife, faced mounting financial difficulties and feared that he was being denied a Top Secret clearance because of indebtedness. Agents found more than 30 past due notices from creditors at his residence showing a total indebtedness of over $25,000. Despite Cavanagh's efforts, it is reported that no serious compromise occurred. According to the prosecuting attorney, had Cavanagh been successful, he would have "gutted" the Stealth Bomber project. Cavanagh pleaded guilty to two counts of espionage and on 23 May 1985 was sentenced to two concurrent life terms in prison.

New York Times	19 Dec 1984, "Engineer is Held in Scheme to Sell Secrets"
Washington Post	22 Dec 1984, "Engineer in Secrets Case is Held Without Bail"

DoD Security Institute, *Security Awareness Bulletin*, Dec 1985, Number 1-86, "Portrait of an Uneasy Spy"

San Francisco Examiner	21 Jun 1987, "Traitor in our Midst"

CHARLTON, JOHN DOUGLAS, retired Lockheed Corporation engineer, was arrested on 25 May 1995 for attempting to sell secret documents removed from the company at the time of his retirement. According to an Assistant US Attorney, the plans concerned the *Sea Shadow*, a Navy stealth project and the *Captor Project* related to mines that release anti-submarine torpedoes. According to the 10-point espionage indictment, Charlton tried to sell the information to an FBI agent posing as a foreign government representative. Five times between July and September 1993, Charlton attempted to sell the secrets for $100,000 to the undercover agent. Charlton joined Lockheed in Sunnyvale, California, in 1980 as a research specialist and left the company under an early retirement program in 1989, but he apparently was disgruntled about the circumstances of his departure. At the time of his retirement he took with him several classified documents outlining US defense projects. A search of his Lancaster, California, residence turned up a cache of illegal guns and the classified documents. Following a plea agreement on 17 October, Charlton pleaded guilty to selling two classified schematic drawings related to the antisubmarine program. He admitted knowing that the *Captor Project* information that the former engineer attempted to sell to what he believed to be a French official was highly classified. According to the prosecuting attorney, "The documents would have enabled any nation to discover some of the workings of the program." On 8 April 1996, Charlton was sentenced to two years in Federal prison and fined $50,000 for his guilty plea to two counts of attempted transfer of defense information. He will be placed on five years' probation after his release. He is not eligible for parole.

Los Angeles Times   26 May 1995, "Ex-Aerospace Worker Indicted In Spy Case"
Antelope Valley Press   18 Oct 1995, "Valley Man Pleads Guilty To Attempted Espionage"
Los Angeles Times   10 Apr 1996, "Retired Engineer Gets 2 Years in Defense Espionage Case"

CHIN, LARRY WU-TAI, retired CIA employee, was arrested 22 November 1985 and accused of having carried out a 33-year career of espionage on behalf of the People's Republic of China. According to media reports, Chin, who retired in 1981 at 63, had been an intelligence officer in the CIA's Foreign Broadcast Information Service. During his career, he held a Top Secret clearance and had access to a wide range of intelligence information. Born in Peking, Chin was recruited by communist intelligence agents while a college student in the early 1940s. He worked for the US Army Liaison Office in China in 1943 and later became a naturalized US citizen, joining the CIA in 1952. It is believed that he provided the PRC with many of the CIA's Top Secret reports on the Far East written over 20 years. Chin reportedly smuggled classified documents from his office, and between 1976 and 1982 gave photographs of these materials to Chinese couriers at frequent meetings in Toronto, Hong Kong, and London. He met with Chinese agents in the Far East up to March 1985, prior to his arrest in November. Chin may have received as much as $1 million for his complicity. He was indicted on 17 counts of espionage-related and income tax violations. It is reported that Chin was identified as a Chinese agent by a Chinese intelligence officer who defected to the US. At his trial which began on 4 February 1986, Chin admitted providing the Chinese with information over a period of 11 years, but he claimed he did so to further reconciliation between China and the US. On 8 February, Chin was convicted by a Federal jury on all counts. Sentencing had been set for 17 March; however, on 21 February the former CIA employee committed suicide in his cell.

Washington Post   24 Nov 1985, "Ex-CIA Employee Held as 33-Year China Spy"
New York Times   30 Nov 1985, "Huge Data Loss from China is Seen from Espionage"
Washington Post   6 Dec 1985, "Chin Believed Planted in US as Spy"
New York Times   11 Feb 1986, "C.I.A.'s Security was Lax, According to Convicted Spy"

CLARK, JAMES MICHAEL, a private investigator, was arrested 4 October 1997 along with **KURT ALLEN STAND** and **THERESE MARIE SQUILLACOTE**, and charged with spying for East Germany. Clark was recruited by his friend Kurt Stand in 1976 when both were members of the Young Workers Liberation League while attending the University of Wisconsin. Media sources state that a 1975 FBI report describing Clark's participation in the youth arm of the Communist party was the basis on which his subsequent application to the CIA for employment was denied. However, in 1986 Clark received a Secret clearance for his work for a private firm doing contract work for the government. And in 1992, the Army renewed his access after hiring him as a civilian analyst. According to news reports, as a defense contractor at the Rocky Mountain Arsenal in Boulder, Colorado, in the 1970s, Clark had access to classified information on chemical warfare. He was also accused of giving East Germany classified State and Commerce Department documents about the Soviet leadership, the Soviet's strategic nuclear doctrine, and problems in the military of Soviet bloc countries. He reportedly told an undercover agent that, under the guise of needing help with a research report, he obtained these classified documents—

including at least one classified as Top Secret—from two State Department employees. Clark admittedly passed information to his German handlers in the form of microfiche. Law enforcement officials and court documents describe Clark as a radical who fell into spying from 1979 to 1989 as an extension of his Marxist ideology. He received at total of $17,500 from East Germany and spent much of it traveling to meet his handler in Germany, Mexico and Canada. Clark was convicted on 3 June 1998 on a charge of conspiracy to commit espionage and on 4 December was sentenced to 12 years and seven months in prison. This reduced sentence was a result of his testimony at the trial of Stand and Squillacote that aided in their conviction. [See also the case summary for Kurt Alan Stand.]

Washington Post	7 Oct 1997, "Three Former Campus Leftists Held in VA on Espionage Charges"
Washington Post	4 Jun 1998, "Falls Church Man Pleads Guilty to Passing Secrets to East Germany"
New York Times	5 Dec 1998, "Spy, in Plea Agreement, Is Given 12-Year Sentence"

CONRAD, CLYDE LEE, retired Army Sergeant First Class, was arrested on 23 August 1988 in West Germany and charged with copying and transmitting classified documents to the Hungarian intelligence service for nearly a decade. He was recruited in 1974 by a Hungarian-born immigrant, **ZOLTAN SZABO**, a veteran of Vietnam who served as an Army Captain in Germany. Szabo began working for Hungarian intelligence in 1967. (He was convicted of espionage by an Austrian court in 1989, but served no jail time because of his cooperation with authorities in the prosecution of Conrad.) Two Hungarian-born doctors arrested at the same time in Sweden are said to have acted as couriers in the espionage operation and Conrad is believed to have hired at least a dozen people in the US Army to supply classified information—one of the biggest spy rings since World War II. Conrad's recruits continued to work for him after returning to the US, illegally exporting hundreds of thousands of advanced computer chips to the East Bloc through a phony company in Canada. In June 1990, former Army sergeant **RODERICK JAMES RAMSAY**, 28, was arrested in Tampa, Florida, following a two-year investigation. Ramsay worked in West Germany from 1983 to 1985 directly under Conrad. He provided Conrad with sensitive documents on the use of tactical nuclear weapons by US forces and NATO allies and plans for the defense of Europe, and manuals on military communications technology. Conrad was granted a Top Secret security clearance in 1978 when assigned to the US 8th Infantry Division headquarters in Bad Kreuznach, Germany. Despite his administrative specialist's job which gave him access to extensive classified materials, Conrad had not been subject to a periodic reinvestigation before his retirement in 1985. Documents provided to Hungarian agents concerned NATO's plans for fighting a war against the Warsaw Pact: detailed descriptions of nuclear weapons and plans for movement of troops, tanks and aircraft. Conrad, in charge of a vault where all the 8th Infantry Division's secret documents were kept, took suitcases stuffed with classified papers out of the base. The former sergeant is reported to have received more than $1 million for selling secrets. The two Hungarian couriers, **SANDOR** and **IMRE KERCSIK** were sentenced by a Swedish court on 18 October to 18 months in prison. In 1989 Conrad was charged with treason under West German law. It took more than a year to charge him formally due to the complexity of the case, which initially was declared one of espionage and then broadened to include the more serious charge of treason. Tried in a West German court, Conrad was sentenced to life imprisonment on 6 June 1990. In January 1998, Conrad died in a German prison, of heart failure.

Washington Post	27 Aug 1988, "US Ex-Sergeant Accused in Spy Case Not Given Mandatory Security Check"
St. Louis Post-Dispatch	2 Sep 1989, "Former US Sergeant Accused of Treason"
Richmond Times-Dispatch	7 Jun 1990, "Former GI Given Life for Spying"
Los Angeles Times	9 Jun 1990, "Alleged Spy Called Brilliant, Erratic"

COOKE, CHRISTOPHER MICHAEL, deputy commander of an Air Force Titan missile crew, was arrested on 21 May 1981 and charged with passing classified information to the Soviets, which seriously compromised US strategic missile capabilities during the 1980-81 time frame. On his own volition, Cooke began to phone and visit the Soviet Embassy in late 1980 with offers to provide classified information. Cooke's motives were never fully established, but it is reported that he was attempting to establish his credentials with the Soviets for the purpose of academic research. It is also known that he sought employment with the CIA on at least two occasions. Believing that Cooke was part of a larger spy ring, Air Force prosecutors offered him immunity from prosecution for a full disclosure. After being given immunity, Cooke admitted to providing classified defense information to the Soviets. The US Court of Military Appeals ordered his release in February 1982 and Cooke resigned his commission.

Washington Post   4 Dec 1983, "Spy Rings of One"
  Magazine

CORDREY, ROBERT ERNEST, a Marine private, was convicted 13 August 1984 by court-martial of 18 counts of attempting to contact representatives of communist countries for the purpose of selling classified information about nuclear, biological and chemical warfare. Cordrey had been an instructor at the Nuclear, Biological and Chemical Defense School at Camp Lejeune, North Carolina. The charges were not contested and the case was not disclosed to the public until January 1985 due to the extremely sensitive nature of the investigation. Apparently Cordrey attempted to contact Soviet, Czech, East German, and Polish agents. While his espionage efforts were thwarted, he attempted to sell classified information for the purpose of making money. He was sentenced to 12 years at hard labor by the military court; however, his pretrial agreement with prosecutors limited his jail term to two years.

New York Times   10 Jan 1985, "Marine Gets 12 Years At Spy Court-Martial"

DAVIES, ALLEN JOHN, former Air Force sergeant and, at the time of his arrest, a laboratory technician at a Silicon Valley defense contractor, was formally charged on 27 October 1986 with trying to pass classified information to the agents of the Soviet Union. Davies, a 10-year veteran who was separated from active service for poor job performance in 1984, had held a Secret clearance during his military service and worked as an avionic sensors system technician. According to the FBI, on 22 September 1986 Davies met with an FBI undercover agent posing as a Soviet official in San Francisco's Golden Gate Park. During the meeting Davies provided detailed verbal information and a hand drawing concerning US reconnaissance technology. At a second meeting in October he provided additional classified information. According to Davies's recorded statement, he was motivated "out of revenge because of the unfair way he was treated while in the Air Force." He is also quoted as saying that he wanted to do something to embarrass the United States and to interfere with the effectiveness of its reconnaissance activities. Asked why he waited two years before providing the information, Davies said he waited "just to make sure they couldn't link me with it if I told anybody, just sort of ... hide my trail." Davies, born in Eastleigh, England in 1953, became a naturalized US citizen at the age of 11. Since October 1984, he had been employed by Ford Aerospace and Communications Corporation in Palo Alto. Federal officials stated that the former airman did not currently hold a clearance and that no information from the contractor facility was involved in the case. Davies was released on $200,000 bail with the condition that he undergo psychological evaluation. But on 27 May 1987 he pleaded guilty to a reduced charge of attempting to communicate secrets to an unauthorized person. Davies was sentenced on 27 August 1987 to five years in prison.

| *Washington Post* | 28 Oct 1986, "FBI Arrests Ex-Airman on Espionage Charges" |
| *Los Angeles Times* | 28 Oct 1986, "San Jose Man Angry at AF Is Arrested as Would-Be Spy" |

DEDEYAN, SADAG K., an employee of the Johns Hopkins Applied Physics Laboratory who was cleared for access to classified information, and a relative, **SARKIS O. PASKALIAN**, were arrested in 1975. Disregarding regulations, Dedeyan had brought home a Top Secret document on NATO defenses to work on. Paskalian, who unbeknownst to Dedeyan, had been recruited and trained by the KGB in 1962, surreptitiously photographed the document and allegedly sold the film to Soviet agents for a reported sum of $1,500. Dedeyan was charged with failing to report the illegal photographing of national defense information. Paskalian was charged with conspiring with Soviet agents to gather and transmit national defense information. Dedeyan was convicted and sentenced to three years. Paskalian pleaded guilty to espionage and was sentenced to 22 years.

Washington Post	28 Jun 1975, "2 Arrested by FBI On Spying Charges "
Washington Post	28 Jun 1975, "Relative Duped Him on Spy Photographs, Accused Man Says"
Washington Post	28 Jun 1975, "Paskalian: Choreographer, Merchant"
New York Times	28 Jun 1975, "2 Held in Plot to Spy for Soviets on NATO"

DESHENG, HOU, a military attaché of the People's Republic of China, was detained by FBI agents on 21 December 1987 while attempting to obtain Secret National Security Agency documents from a Federal employee. Desheng was taken into custody at a restaurant in Washington's Chinatown after accepting what he believed to be classified NSA documents. The Federal employee, a US citizen, had been working under FBI direction. Arrested at the same time was **ZANG WEICHU,** a PRC consular official in Chicago. Both diplomats were asked to leave the country as a result of "activities incompatible with their diplomatic status" – the first Chinese diplomats expelled since formal relations were established with the PRC in 1979.

| *New York Times* | 31 Dec 1987, "2 Chinese Depart in Espionage Case" |
| *Washington Post* | 31 Dec 1987, "US Expels Two Chinese Diplomats as Spies" |

DIAZ, MATTHEW M., a staff attorney with the US Navy Judge Advocate General's Corps, was charged in August 2006 with the unauthorized disclosure of the names of the 551 Guantanamo Bay detainees while stationed there as a Navy lawyer. After some two weeks of indecision, he had mailed— between December 2004 and March 2005—to a civil rights attorney in New York the classified names, months before the Department of Defense was eventually forced to release the same names as a result of Freedom of Information requests. The civil rights attorney in New York turned over the file to the FBI whose agents tracked down Diaz and arrested him on charges of five felony counts, including the disclosure of classified information that could aid American foreign enemies. The Supreme Court had upheld the Guantanamo prisoners' rights to challenge their detention in habeas corpus proceedings, but six months later the government was still challenging the court's order, insisting the prisoners had no legal rights and certainly no right to counsel. Pentagon officials said they were keeping prisoners' names secret for the prisoners' own protection, but this made it difficult for potential defense attorneys to file petitions on their behalf. Tried by military court-martial in May 2007, Diaz was convicted of violating orders by passing classified information that could be used to harm the US to someone outside the government. He was sentenced on 17 May to six months' confinement and was later stripped of his license to practice military law.

Jurist Legal News & Research   30 Oct 2006, "Navy Postpones Hearing for Gitmo Military Lawyer Accused of
Leaking Detainee Names"
New York Times   21 Oct 2007, "Naming Names at Gitmo"

DOLCE, THOMAS JOSEPH, civilian research analyst at Aberdeen Proving Ground, Maryland, admitted in Federal court on 11 October 1988 that he had supplied scores of Secret documents related to Soviet military equipment to the Republic of South Africa between 1979 and 1983. Dolce, who had been under investigation by the FBI since April, resigned from his position on 30 September "for personal reasons." Dolce had held a Secret clearance at the Army Material Systems Analysis Activity at Aberdeen where he had been employed since 1973. In pleading guilty to a single count of espionage, he acknowledged passing documents on 40 or more occasions by mail or in person to military attachés at the South African Embassy in Washington and at South African Missions in London and Los Angeles. According to Dolce, he was motivated by ideological rather than financial reasons and had a long-term interest in the Republic of South Africa. He had in fact moved to South Africa in 1971, but later returned to the US because of better employment opportunities. Prior to 1971 Dolce had been a US Army clandestine warfare specialist. His contacts with South African representatives began when he sent them an unclassified paper on clandestine warfare that he had written. There is no evidence that Dolce received money in exchange for documents. On 20 April 1989, the former analyst was sentenced to 10 years in prison and fined $5,000.

Washington Post   12 Oct 1988, "Md. Man Admits to Espionage for South Africa"
Washington Post   13 Oct 1988, "Spy for S. Africa Called Reserved"

DUBBERSTEIN, WALDO H., retired DIA employee and associate of convicted arms smuggler Edwin P. Wilson, was indicted on 28 April 1983 on charges of selling US military secrets to Libya. The following day Dubberstein was found dead; his death was later ruled a suicide. Had he been convicted of espionage and of other charges against him, including conspiracy and bribery, Dubberstein would have faced a possible sentence of 57 years and $80,000 in fines. Dubberstein had apparently begun his cooperation with Libya as an outgrowth of meetings with an old CIA friend, Edwin P. Wilson, who acted as a middleman for passage of information to Libya and receipt of payments to Dubberstein.

Washington Post   8 May 1983, "The Last Battle of an Old War Horse"
Time   9 May 1983, "Beyond Justice: An Accused Spy is Dead"

ELLIS, ROBERT WADE, Navy Petty Officer, stationed at the Naval Air Station, Moffett Field, California, reportedly contacted the Soviet Consulate in San Francisco, with an offer to sell classified documents for $2,000. Ellis, who had clearly wanted to make money by his espionage activities, was arrested in February 1983 while attempting to sell documents to an undercover FBI agent. He was convicted at a general court-martial for unauthorized disclosure of classified information and was sentenced to three years' confinement.

ENGER, VALDIK and **RUDOLF CHERNYAYEV**, both Soviet employees of the UN Secretariat, were arrested by the FBI in New Jersey in May 1978 for accepting classified information on antisubmarine warfare passed by a US Naval officer acting on instructions of the Naval Investigative Service and the FBI. The officer, Navy Lieutenant Commander Art Lindberg, acted as a double agent in a counterintelligence operation called Operation Lemonaid. In August 1977, LCDR Lindberg took a trip on the Soviet cruise ship *Kazakhstan*. Upon the ship's return to New York, he passed a note to one of the

Soviet officers containing an offer to sell information. He was later contacted by telephone by a Soviet agent. During subsequent telephone calls, LCDR Lindberg was given contact instructions on the type of information to get and the locations of drop sites where that information could be left and payment money could be found. Naval Investigative Service and FBI agents kept the drop zones under surveillance and later identified the Soviet agents. On 20 May 1978, FBI agents moved into the drop zone and apprehended three Soviets, Enger, Chernyayev and another man, **VLADIMIR ZINYAKIN**, third secretary at the Soviet Mission to the United Nations. Zinyakin avoided arrest due to diplomatic immunity. Enger and Chernyayev, the first Soviet officials ever to stand trial for espionage in the US, were convicted and sentenced to 50 years in prison. Altogether they paid the Navy officer $16,000 for materials he provided. Enger and Chernyayev were later exchanged for the release of five Soviet dissidents.

New York Times	21 May 1978, "2 Russians Arrested by F.B.I. for Spying"
Washington Post	24 Dec 1978, "The Spy Who Came Into The Cold"
Los Angeles Times	24 May 1979, "Navy Officer 'Drafted' as Counterspy"

Naval Investigative Service Command, *Espionage*, 1989

FAGET, MARIANO, a high-ranking Immigration and Naturalization Service official in Miami, Florida, was arrested on 17 February 2000 for providing classified information to the Cuban intelligence service. Faget is a naturalized citizen who had migrated to the US in 1959. At the time of his arrest he held a Secret security clearance and had access to sensitive INS files. He first became a suspect in 1999 when technical and physical surveillance indicated that he was making unauthorized contacts with known Cuban agents. His arrest the following year was based on an FBI sting operation in which Faget was shown (bogus) information that a Cuban diplomat was about to defect. A few minutes later, the INS official was recorded passing this information by phone to a business contact with ties to Cuban intelligence. A member of the Cuban mission, who had been a contact for Faget, was declared persona non grata and expelled. It is not known how much information Faget may have provided the Cuban intelligence service during his years with the INS. Following his arraignment on 3 March 2000, he pleaded not guilty to charges of disclosing classified information, converting it for his own gain, lying to the FBI about contact with a Cuban official, and failing to disclose foreign business ties on his security clearance application. On 30 May 2000, Faget was convicted on all four counts. Prosecutors stated that Faget's motives were financial gain rather than political. He had expectations of engaging in a lucrative trading business with Cuba once the US embargo is lifted. The former INS official was sentenced on 29 June 2001 to five years in prison including the 16 months in custody at the time of sentencing. His 35 years of otherwise exemplary service to the INS were noted by the judge.

Miami Herald	12 Mar 2000, "Faget: 'Spy' Talk Was Only Business"
New York Times	31 May 2000, "I.N.S. Official Is Convicted on Charges of Espionage"
Miami Herald	30 Jun 2001, "INS Official Gets 5 Years in Spy Sting"

FLEMING, DAVID, Navy Chief Petty Officer, was convicted by a six-member military court on 4 October 1988 for the theft of 16 Secret photographs and four classified training manuals that he had at his home. At the time of his arrest in October 1987, Fleming was chief photographer aboard the submarine *La Jolla*, based at San Diego, California. At that time Federal agents found classified material in Fleming's apartment. Fleming contended that cramped quarters aboard the ship led him to develop photographs at home. Concluding that he knew that the materials, if kept at home, could result in damage to national security, the court convicted Fleming under statutes which apply to acts of espionage. However, no evidence was presented to the court that the Chief Petty Officer had intended to provide classified materials to representatives of another country. Fleming was sentenced to four years' confinement and was given a bad conduct discharge from the Navy. In April 1989 a Navy parole board in San Diego recommended that the remainder of the four-year sentence be commuted. He was released on parole in 1990.

Los Angeles Times	5 Oct 1988, "Sailor Gets Prison in Classified Data Case"
San Diego Union	15 Apr 1989, "Early Release Backed for Sailor Convicted on Security Charges

FORBRICH, ERNST, a West German automobile mechanic, was arrested 19 March 1984 in Clearwater Beach, Florida, after paying $550 for a classified military document supplied by an undercover agent posing as an Army intelligence officer. Forbrich was described as a conduit who passed US military secrets to East German intelligence and by his own admission had been selling documents to East German intelligence for a period of 17 years. Forbrich traveled frequently to the US, contacting former US military personnel who had served in West Germany. Convicted in June on two counts of espionage, Forbrich was sentenced to 15 years.

Washington Post	21 Mar 1984, "West German Accused of Spying for East"
New York Times	21 Mar 1984, "German is Arrested on Spying Charge"

FORD, KENNETH WAYNE, JR., employed as a computer expert by the National Security Agency (NSA) from June 2001 until late 2003, was arrested on 12 January 2004 and accused of taking national security documents without authorization. On the last day of his employment at NSA, Ford packed cardboard boxes with highly classified documents, left through an unguarded exit, and loaded the boxes into his vehicle. Acting on his then-girlfriend's tip, FBI agents executed a search warrant for Ford's home in Waldorf, Maryland, and discovered sensitive classified information stashed throughout the house, including Top Secret documents in two boxes in the kitchen. Ford was arrested the same day. Prosecutors did not allege that Ford took the documents to give or sell to a foreign government, and Ford claimed that he stole the documents because he thought they would help him get a new job with Northrop Grumman. However, he did not get the job and a few months later, a federal judge told Ford that if he applied for any other job requiring a security clearance, he must divulge that he had been charged with unlawfully possessing national security documents. Ford did subsequently apply to Lockheed Martin but failed to disclose on the government clearance form the charges pending against him regarding the theft from NSA. Ford was convicted in December 2005 after a two-week trial for unlawful possession of classified information and making a false statement to a US government agency. On 26 March 2006, he was sentenced to six years in prison, followed by three years' supervised release.

Washingtonpost.com	30 Nov 2005, "Md. Man on Trial Over NSA Documents"
U.S. Attorney's Office,	30 Mar 2006, "Former Maryland NSA Employee Sentenced for Wrongfully
District of MD Press Blog	Possessing Classified Information"
FBI Headline Archives (fbi.gov)	31 Mar 2006, "You Can't Take It With You: Maryland Man Sentenced for
	Stealing Secret Documents"

FRANKLIN, LAWRENCE ANTHONY, an intelligence analyst in the Office of the Secretary of Defense, International Security Affairs, Iran desk, held a Top Secret clearance with access to sensitive compartmented information. The FBI filed criminal charges against Franklin 3 May 2005, accusing him of passing, from 2002 to 2004, classified military information about Iran and Iraq to two pro-Israel lobbyists, Steven Rosen and Keith Weissman, and to an Israeli diplomat. Rosen and Weissman were senior staff members of the American Israel Public Affairs Committee (AIPAC), a pro-Israel lobbying organization. Their own prosecution in the same case was novel in that neither held security clearances that required them to protect U.S. classified information. Franklin pleaded guilty in October 2005 to three felony counts in exchange for his cooperation and the government's willingness to drop three other charges. He was sentenced in January 2006 to 12 years and seven months in prison and a $10,000 fine. This relatively lenient sentence reflected the judge's impression that Franklin had been driven by a desire to help, not damage, the US. Franklin was not to begin his sentence until after legal proceedings against Rosen and Weissman were completed, at which time his sentence might be reduced. Meanwhile, Franklin remained free on bail. On 1 May 2009 prosecutors announced that they were abandoning the charges against Rosen and Weissman and then, on 12 June 2009, Franklin's sentence was reduced to probation, with 10 months of home confinement.

BBCnews.com	20 Jan 2006, "Pentagon Man Jailed Over Spying"
New York Times	1 Dec 2006, "Former Military Analyst Gets Prison Term for Passing Information"
Federation of American Scientists	23 Jun 2008, "Court Narrows Scope of Appeal in AIPAC Case"
Washington Post	1 May 2009, "Charges to be Dropped Against Two Former AIPAC Lobbyists"
Washington Post	12 Jun 2009, "Sentence Reduced in Pentagon Case"

GARCIA, WILFREDO, Navy Master-at-Arms 1st Class, was found guilty of espionage on 22 January 1988 following a two-year investigation by agents of the Naval Investigative Service and the FBI. In late 1985, NIS and FBI officials received information that a civilian businessman in Vallejo, California, was attempting to sell classified Navy documents to representatives of a foreign government. A cooperating witness identified Garcia, who was then stationed at Mare Island Naval Shipyard, as the source. Confidential documents stolen by Garcia dealing with submarine activities were sold to the civilian for $800,000, with a promise of more money when they were resold to a foreign government. Evidence indicated that the final destination could have been an East-Bloc country. The espionage scheme resulted in a number of classified documents being taken to the Philippines for sale to a foreign power there. Participants in the conspiracy couriered the documents on commercial aircraft and had gathered the material in a residence in Manila. NIS agents in Manila entered the home with a search warrant and recovered the documents before the planned sale. At a general court-martial convened in January 1988, Garcia was found guilty of espionage, conspiracy to commit espionage, larceny, conspiracy to commit larceny, sale of government property, and violations of military regulations. He was sentenced to 12 years' confinement, reduced in rank to E-1, forfeited all pay and allowances, and received a dishonorable discharge from the Navy. Garcia had served in the Navy for 15 years.

Naval Investigative Service Command, *Espionage*, 1989
Sentry   Spring/Summer 1988, "MA1 Convicted of Espionage"

GILBERT, OTTO ATTILA, Hungarian-born US citizen, was arrested 17 April 1982 after paying $4,000 for classified documents provided by an Army officer who was working as a US Army double agent under Army control. The officer, CWO Janos Szmolka, had been approached in 1977 by agents of Hungarian military intelligence while on a visit to his mother in Hungary and had reported the contact to Army intelligence. While stationed in Europe, Szmolka agreed to work as a double agent. In 1981 he received $3,000 for 16 rolls of film of unclassified documents and was offered $100,000 for classified material on weapon and cryptographic systems. Szmolka was reassigned to Fort Gordon, Georgia, in 1980, but maintained his contacts with Hungarian intelligence, which led to the meeting with Gilbert. Gilbert was convicted of espionage and sentenced to 15 years in prison. This case is considered to be a classic example of recruitment based on a hostage situation since implied threats were made against the Hungarian relations of the US service member.

Washington Post   20 Apr 1982, "Spying is Charged to New Yorker of Hungarian Origin"
New York Times   20 Apr 1982, "Native of Hungary is Jailed in South on Spying Charges"

GREGORY, JEFFERY EUGENE, a US Army Staff Sergeant was arrested 29 April 1993 at Fort Richardson, Alaska, resulting from a joint investigation between the FBI and the US Army Intelligence and Security Command. Gregory was one of several members of a spy ring operating out of the 8th Infantry Division, Bad Kreuznach, Germany, in the mid-1980s that sold US and NATO military secrets to Hungary and Czechoslovakia when those countries were in the Soviet Bloc. German authorities convicted the ring-leader, former US Army sergeant **CLYDE LEE CONRAD**, of high treason in 1990 and sentenced him to life in prison. In 1991, another ring member **RODERICK JAMES RAMSAY**, also a former Army sergeant stationed in Bad Kreuznach, was sentenced to 36 years in prison by an American court for his involvement in the network. Clyde Conrad recruited Ramsay who is believed to have then recruited others, including Gregory. According to the Federal complaint against Gregory, while assigned to the 8th Infantry Division in Germany from March 1984 to October 1986, "he helped procure extremely sensitive, classified documents relating to national defense, for transmittal to one or more foreign powers." At that time, Gregory was a staff driver at Bad Kreuznach, West Germany, and helped maintain the commanding general's mobile command center. He was also in charge of updating maps showing military maneuvers and had access to classified messages and correspondence. According to an FBI official, Gregory once took a military flight bag stuffed with 20 pounds of classified documents. The documents included "war plans" for the US and NATO. On 28 March 1994, Gregory pleaded guilty to espionage charges. In June, 1994, Gregory, along with Sgt. **JEFFREY STEPHEN RONDEAU**, another member of the espionage ring, was sentenced by a military court to 18 years in prison.

New York Times   2 May 1993, "Fourth Army Sergeant Held in Espionage Case"
Huntsville Times   2 May 1993, "4th Army Sgt. Arrested in Alleged Espionage Ring in Germany"

GROAT, DOUGLAS FREDERICK, former CIA officer, was arrested on 3 April 1998 and charged with passing sensitive intelligence information to two foreign governments and attempting to extort over $500,000 from the CIA in return for not disclosing additional secrets. Groat had been placed on a three-year paid administrative leave in the spring of 1993 after the agency felt he posed a security risk, reportedly involving a discipline or job performance issue. Apparently Groat first attempted to extort money from the CIA in May 1996 and was fired the following October. During a 16-year career at the CIA, Groat participated in intelligence operations aimed at penetrating the secret codes and communication systems employed by foreign governments. Groat, a cryptographic expert, was reported to have revealed classified information to two undisclosed governments regarding the targeting and compromise of their cryptographic systems in March and April 1997. For Groat, it was "very much a case of pure revenge," said a Federal official, explaining that the former intelligence officer had long felt slighted and abused by the CIA because he had never been given the assignments he thought he deserved. Groat is reported to have not received any money from the foreign governments for the information passed. The former CIA employee pleaded guilty to one count of attempted extortion 27 July, and was sentenced 27 September to five years' confinement followed by three years' probation. According to news reports, the sharp reduction from the original four-count espionage charge and the limited penalties reflected the government's desire to avoid a trial in which damaging classified information might have been disclosed.

Washington Times   4 Apr 1998, "Former CIA Officer Charged With Spying; Pleads Not guilty in Extortion, Codes Case"
Washington Post   28 Jul 1998, "Ex-CIA Operative Pleads Guilty to Blackmail Attempt at Agency"

GUERRERO, ANTONIO, part of the Cuban Red Wasp Network spy ring in south Florida, was born in Miami where his father, a professional baseball player, was working. [See also Linda Hernandez, Gerardo Hernandes, Joseph Santos, and Alejandro Alonso.] The family returned to Cuba where Antonio grew up and was recruited by the Cuban Intelligence Service. He began spying for Cuba in Panama in 1991, then was sent to the US in 1992 and tasked with collecting visual intelligence against the Boca Chica Naval Air Station in Key West, Florida. Guerrero, 43, got a job doing maintenance and construction work on the base. He passed coded reports on activities at the naval air station, such as plane counts, base remodeling, or changes of command, which could indicate an impending US invasion of Cuba. He passed his information to the head of the ring, **GERARDO HERNANDEZ**. Although he and two of his fellow agents in south Florida had no clearances and obtained no classified information, they were successfully prosecuted for conspiracy to commit espionage. On 27 December 2001, Guerrero was sentenced to life in prison for conspiracy to commit espionage and for acting as an unregistered agent of a foreign government.

Washington Post	15 Sep 1998, "10 Arrested on Charges of Spying for Cuba"
South Florida Sun-Sentinel	31 Dec 2000, "Exile's Dual Life Begets Federal Spying Charge"
Guardian (UK)	6 Mar 2001, "Carry on Spying"

HAGUEWOOD, ROBERT DEAN, Petty Officer 3rd Class, was arrested 4 March 1986 by agents of the Naval Investigative Service after allegedly selling part of a Confidential aviation ordinance manual to an undercover police officer. Haguewood, who was stationed at the Pacific Missile Test Center at Point Mugu Naval Air Station near Oxnard, California, reportedly asked around town for someone who would pay for secret information about Naval ordinance. He was placed under surveillance by agents of the Naval Investigative Service who, with the FBI and local police officials, made the arrest on 4 March after Haguewood received a payment of $360 for the classified document at a beach location. No contact was made with foreign representatives and no information is known to have been compromised. Haguewood was reported to have had serious financial problems. On 20 June, Haguewood pleaded guilty under a plea-bargain agreement and received a sentence of two years from a military court.

Washington Post	1 Mar 1986, "Sailor Allegedly Tried to Sell Manual"
New York Times	11 Mar 1986, "Navy Man Arrested in Spy Case"
Washington Post	20 Jun 1986, "Sale of 'Secrets' To Put Sailor Behind Bars"

HALL, JAMES III, Army Warrant Officer, was arrested on 21 December 1988 in Savannah, Georgia, after bragging to an undercover FBI agent that over a period of six years he had sold Top Secret intelligence data to East Germany and the Soviet Union. At the time, Hall believed that he was speaking to a Soviet contact. During this conversation he claimed that he had been motivated only by money. He told the FBI agent posing as a Soviet intelligence officer, "I wasn't terribly short of money. I just decided I didn't ever want to worry where my next dollar was coming from. I'm not anti-American. I wave the flag as much as anybody else." Also arrested, in Bellaire, Florida, was **HUSEYIN YILDIRIM** (nicknamed "the Meister"), a Turkish national who served as a conduit between Hall and East German agents. He was working as a civilian mechanic at an Army auto shop in Germany at the time. According to FBI sources, Hall started passing documents to East German agents in 1982 while serving in West Berlin as a communications analyst monitoring East Bloc cable traffic. Later, Hall was transferred to Frankfurt where he continued to pass "massive amounts" of highly classified data on communications intelligence. Hall is believed to have received over $100,000 from agents of two countries during this period of time. In July 1987 he was reassigned to Ft. Stewart, near Savannah, Georgia. Hall had been under investigation by FBI and Army counterintelligence agents for several months before his arrest and had been observed meeting Yildirim three times in November and December. Hall's detection as an espionage source may have resulted from reports that Hall was living in a style far above what his pay scale would allow. According to US officials, the operation appears to have inflicted serious damage on US electronic intelligence collection activities in Europe. On 9 March 1989 Hall was sentenced to 40 years in prison, fined $50,000 and given a dishonorable discharge. Yildirim was convicted 20 July 1989 of scheming with Hall and sentenced to life. Prosecutors contended that from 1982 to 1988 Yildirim carried classified military intelligence from Hall to East Bloc agents and returned with money.

New York Times	22 Dec 1988, "Army Technician and a Civilian are Held as Spies for Soviet Bloc
Washington Post	23 Dec 1988, "Spy Suspect Said to Act Prosperous"
New York Times	19 Jul 1989, "Jury Hears Tale of Spy Who Did It Out of Greed"
Newsweek	2 Jan 1989, "Top Secrets for Sale?"

HAMILTON, FREDERICK CHRISTOPHER, a former Defense Intelligence Agency official, pleaded guilty on 5 February 1993 to the charge of passing to Ecuadorian officials classified US intelligence reports evaluating the military readiness of Peruvian security forces. At the time, Hamilton was a DIA research technician in the defense attaché's office in Lima, Peru, a post which he held from 1989 to 1991. He apparently believed that the disclosures could help avert a possible conflict between the two countries. Peru and Ecuador have been disputing territory (sometimes violently) along their mutual border for the past 50 years. Hamilton holds advanced degrees in Spanish and Portuguese. At the time of his arrest, he was employed as a language instructor at a military academy in Virginia. His activities were uncovered by US intelligence agencies after they received information from a confidential source indicating secrets were being leaked. Hamilton, who held a Top Secret security clearance while with the DIA, met Ecuadorian representatives in their embassy in Lima on 13 February and 20 May of 1991. He passed extremely sensitive information that disclosed US intelligence operations and the identity of US sources in the region. "He didn't get any money," said a US official. "He was a very naive individual who was flattered by the [Ecuadorians]." Hamilton's attorney stated that, "What he thought he was trying to do was prevent a war... The purpose of disclosing the documents that he did was to show the country that was concerned about being attacked that the other country had neither the intent nor the ability to attack." Hamilton reportedly passed five Secret intelligence reports and orally disclosed the contents of four other classified reports. Under a court agreement, the former DIA employee pleaded guilty to two counts of unlawfully communicating classified information to a foreign country. The agreement specifies Hamilton may not appeal the sentence and the Justice Department will not prosecute him for espionage-related crimes. On 16 April, he was sentenced to 37 months in prison.

Washington Post	6 Feb 1993, "Va. Man Pleads Guilty to Leaking US Secrets"
Washington Times	6 Feb 1993, "Ex-DIA Official Pleads Guilty in Document Leak"

HANSSEN, ROBERT PHILIP, an agent for the FBI for 27 years, was charged on 20 February 2001 with spying for Russia for more than 15 years. He was arrested in a park near his home in Vienna, Virginia, as he dropped off a bag containing seven Secret documents at a covert location. For most of his FBI career Hanssen had worked in counterintelligence, and he made use of what he learned in his own espionage career. He was charged with espionage and conspiracy to commit espionage. Specifically, Hanssen provided first the Soviets and then the Russian government over 6,000 pages of classified documents and the identities of three Russian agents working for the US. Two of these sources were tried in Russia and executed. According to court documents, the FBI employee provided information on "some of the most sensitive and highly compartmented projects in the US intelligence community" as well as details on US nuclear war defenses. In return, the Russians paid him $1.4 million over the period of his espionage activities, including over $600,000 in cash and diamonds and $800,000 deposited in a Russian bank account. Hanssen was identified after the US obtained his file from a covert source in the Russian intelligence service. However, the Russians never knew Hanssen's true name. To them, he was known only as "Ramon" or "Garcia." It is believed that Hanssen was involved with the Soviets beginning in 1979, broke off the relationship in 1980, but again volunteered to engage in espionage in 1985 by sending an unsigned letter to a KGB officer in the Soviet Embassy in Washington. The letter included the names of the three Soviet double-agents working in the US. Although Hanssen's motives are unclear, they seem to have included ego gratification, disgruntlement with his job at the FBI, and a need for money. He and his wife struggled to provide for their large family on an agent's salary and by 1992 had incurred debts of over $275,000. Hanssen exploited the FBI's computer systems for classified information to sell and kept tabs on possible investigations of himself by accessing FBI computer files. Friends and coworkers were at a loss to explain how this supposedly deeply religious father of six and ardent anti-Communist could have been leading a double life. A large part of his illegal income is believed to have been used to buy expensive gifts and a car for a local stripper. In July 2001, a plea agreement was reached by which Hanssen would plead guilty to espionage, fully cooperate with investigators, but avoid the death penalty. On 11 May 2002, the former FBI agent was sentenced to life in prison.

New York Times	21 Feb 2001, "F.B.I. Agent Charged as Spy Who Aided Russia for 15 Years"
Washington Post	25 Feb 2001, "'A Question of Why,' Contradictory Portrait Emerges of Spying Suspect"
Washington Post	6 Jan 2002, "From Russia with Love"
Los Angeles Times	7 May 2002, "U.S. Authorities Question FBI Spy's Candor"

HARPER, JAMES DURWARD, a Silicon Valley freelance electrical engineer, was arrested 15 October 1983 for selling large quantities of classified documents to Polish intelligence for a reported sum of $250,000. Harper, who did not hold a clearance, acquired classified material through his wife, **RUBY SCHULER**. Schuler was employed as secretary to the president of Systems Control, Inc. of Palo Alto, a defense contractor engaged in research on ballistic missiles. She allowed Harper to come into the Systems Control offices on weekends and at night to copy documents that were subsequently passed to Polish intelligence agents. Between July 1979 and November 1981, Harper conducted a total of a dozen meetings with Polish agents in Europe and Mexico at which he turned over documents related to the Minuteman ICBM and ballistic missile research. While Harper seems to have been motivated by money, Schuler passed along classified documents in an effort to please Harper. Less than three weeks before she died, Schuler told a close friend: "There is a reason that Jim and I got married that only he and I know. I can't tell you or anyone else and I never will." In September 1981 Harper, beginning to regret his behavior, attempted to bargain for immunity from prosecution by anonymously contacting the CIA through a lawyer. Schuler died in June 1983 of complications related to alcoholism. Harper, who eventually pleaded guilty to six counts of espionage, received a life sentence on 14 May 1984.

| *Washington Post* | 18 Oct 1983, "KGB Intelligence 'Windfall'" |
| *Time Magazine* | 31 Oct 1983, "For Love of Money and Adventure" |

DoD Security Institute, *Security Awareness Bulletin,* No. 4-84, August 1984, "Partners in Espionage: The Case of James Harper and Ruby Louise Schuler"

HAWKINS, STEPHEN DWAYNE, was serving in 1985 as a Quartermaster Third Class at the Commander Submarine Group 8 in Naples, Italy. A visitor to his home off base in June reported seeing a classified message there. Interviews with Hawkins by Naval Investigative Service agents and a series of polygraphs that showed deception resulted in Hawkins confessing that he had taken at least 17 Secret messages home with him and was considering selling them to a hostile intelligence service. He was convicted at general court-martial on 15 January 1986 of violating Article 92, wrongful removal of classified material and wrongful destruction of a classified message. He was sentenced to a dishonorable discharge, one year in prison, and reduction in grade to E-1.

Naval Investigative Service Command, *Espionage*, 1989

HELMICH, JOSEPH GEORGE, a former US Army Warrant Officer, was arrested on 15 July 1981 at his residence in Jacksonville, Florida, for the sale of US cryptography to the Soviet Union from 1963 to 1966. Helmich served as a crypto custodian in France and at Ft. Bragg, North Carolina. He initiated contact with USSR embassy officials in Paris after being faced with severe financial problems. In return for extremely sensitive information related to the KL-7 cryptographic system widely used by the US military, Helmich received approximately $131,000. After being transferred to Ft. Bragg, Helmich continued to provide the Soviets with KL-7 key lists and traveled to both France and Mexico City to rendezvous with his handlers. Helmich came under suspicion in 1964 and was questioned because of his unexplained affluence. He was interviewed again in August 1980 and, although admitting he had received $20,000 from Soviet agents, denied he had compromised classified information. In early 1981 he was spotted with Soviet agents in Canada. Eventually Helmich recounted full details of his espionage involvement. On 16 October 1981, he was sentenced to life imprisonment.

Washington Post	16 Jul 1981, "Ex-Army Cryptographer Indicted on Spy Charges"
New York Times	16 Jul 1981, "Ex-Army Warrant Officer Accused of Being Soviet Spy"
New York Times	24 Sep 1981, "Generals Testify in Espionage Case"

HERNANDEZ, GERARDO, a captain in the Cuban military intelligence, was also spymaster of an extensive ring of Cuban nationals and Cuban Americans collecting intelligence, attempting to commit espionage and disrupt Cuban exile groups in south Florida from 1992 until 1998. On 12 September 1998 the FBI arrested 10 people associated with the "La Red Avispa," or the Red Wasp Network ring, including eight men and two women in their various south Florida residences. They were accused of spying on US military installations and anti-Castro exile groups in south Florida and transmitting this information to Cuba. Among the military installations the group attempted to infiltrate were the US Southern Command Headquarters in Miami, MacDill Air Force Base near Tampa, and Boca Chica Naval Air Station in Key West. The group's goals included documenting activities, exercises, and trends at the installations; monitoring anti-Castro groups and disrupting their plans; and developing positions of vantage from which to warn Cuban intelligence of impending military strikes against Cuba. The group had been under investigation by the FBI counterintelligence squad in Miami since 1995.

Three of the 10 arrested were identified as senior agents who communicated directly with Cuban intelligence officials and received their instructions from Cuba. The three senior agents were all Cuban nationals. They were **GERARDO HERNANDEZ**, 31 (alias Manuel Viramontes), the spymaster; **FERNANDO GONZALEZ**, 33 (alias Ruben Campa), and **RAMON LABANINO**, 30 (alias Luis Medina), another Cuban intelligence officer. The remaining seven were mid-level or junior agents who passed their reports to one of these three senior agents. Included were **ANTONIO GUERRERO**, 39, who observed aircraft landings at the Boca Chica Naval Air Station from his job as a sheet-metal worker there; **ALEJANDRO ALONSO**, 39, a boat pilot; and **RENE GONZALEZ**, 42, a skilled aircraft pilot and the only Cuban national among these seven. Both joined the Democracy Movement to report on its activities devoted to harassing the Castro government with demonstrations and threats. Two married couples, all American citizens, also worked in the spy network: **NILO** and **LINDA HERNANDEZ**, ages

44 and 41 respectively, and **JOSEPH** and **AMARYLIS SANTOS**, both 39. Five defendants, Alonzo, the Hernandez's, and the Santos's, accepted a plea bargain and cooperated with the prosecutors, providing information about the others. The other five defendants eventually went to trial, which lasted six months.

The US government's espionage case also became enmeshed with an incident that happened in February 1996, in which Cuban air force jets shot down two of three Cessna aircraft flying toward Havana. Four pilots, members of the anti-Castro exile group, Brothers to the Rescue, were killed. Several of the Wasp network agents had infiltrated Brothers to the Rescue, including Rene Gonzalez, the pilot. In addition to charges related to information-gathering and the sending of "nonpublic" information to a foreign power, Gerardo Hernandez was charged with contributing to the deaths of the four pilots for passing along to Cuban intelligence information about the group's planned fly-over. Several other Cubans who were eventually indicted in the incident fled to Cuba before they could be arrested.

The trial of the five Wasp defendants who had not entered into plea bargains resulted in convictions on all counts on 8 June 2001. Three received life sentences in December 2001 for conspiracy to commit espionage, although they did not collect or compromise any classified information. Cuban nationals, Gerardo Hernandez and Ramon Labanino, and Antonio Guerrero, an American citizen, received life in prison. Fernando Gonzalez and Rene Gonzalez, also Cuban nationals, received sentences of 19 years and 10 years, respectively, for conspiracy and for acting as unregistered agents of a foreign power. The five American citizens who pled guilty to one count of acting as unregistered agents of a foreign power received lesser sentences: Alejandro Alonso, Nilo Hernandez, and Linda Hernandez got sentences of seven years' imprisonment, Joseph Santos received four years, and Amarylis Santos three and a half.

Washington Post	15 Sep 1998, "10 Arrested on Charges of Spying for Cuba"
Fort Lauderdale Sun-Sentinel	8 May 1999, "Cuban Spies Linked to Shoot-down"
Miami Herald	16 Aug 1999, "Shadowing of Cubans a Classic Spy Tale"
Guardian (UK)	6 Mar 2001, "Carry on Spying"
Miami Times	15 Mar 2001, "What Spies Beneath"
Associated Press	30 Dec 2001, "Cuban Parliament Declares Five Agents 'Heroes of Cuba'"

HERNANDEZ, LINDA 43, and her husband **NILO HERNANDEZ**, 46, were members of the Wasp Network, a Cuban spy ring in south Florida. Linda was born in New York but returned to Cuba where she grew up and married Nilo. In 1983 the couple returned to the US where he later became an American citizen. In 1992 they were "activated" as spies and ordered to move from New York to Miami. They were arrested on 12 September 1998 along with eight other members of the ring. [See also Gerardo Hernandez and Alejandro Alonso.] Linda was charged with attempting to collect information for the Cuban Intelligence Service by infiltrating a right-wing Cuban exile group called Alpha 66. Nilo counted aircraft at nearby Homestead Air Force Base and reported using a shortwave radio. Although the information they passed to Cuba was in the public domain, in a plea bargain, the pair pled guilty to acting as unregistered agents of a foreign government. Each was sentenced to seven years in prison in US District court in Miami on 23 February 2000.

Miami Herald	8 Feb 1998, "Cuban Couple Pleads Guilty in Spying Case"
Miami Herald	24 Feb 2000, "Confessed Cuban Spies Sentenced to Seven Years"

HERRMANN, RUDOLPH ALBERT, KGB career officer, entered the US illegally with his family from Canada in 1968 and operated as a Soviet agent within the US under the guise of a free-lance photographer. His primary assignment was to gather political information. While Herrmann claimed not to have recruited Americans for espionage, he admitted to having transmitted sensitive information collected by other spies and to acting as a courier for the KGB. Apprehended by the FBI in 1977, he agreed to operate as a double agent until the operation was terminated in 1980. Herrmann and his family were granted asylum in the US have been resettled under a new identity.

New York Times   4 Mar 1980, "Double Agent Revealed by FBI"
Washington Post   4 Mar 1980, "Soviet Spy Became a 'Double Agent'
John Barron, *The Inheritor: A Tale of KGB Espionage in America*, 1982

HOFFMAN, RONALD, was working as a general manager at Science Applications International Corporation (SAIC), in Century City, California, when his dissatisfaction with his salary led him to create a sideline business called "Plume Technology" at home. Hoffman had worked on a software program called CONTAM, developed at SAIC under classified contract for the Air Force, which could classify rockets upon launch from their exhaust contrails and respond with appropriate countermeasures. The software also had application for the design of spacecraft, guided missiles, and launch vehicles. In 1986 he contacted Japanese companies working with Japan's space program and offered to sell them entire CONTAM modules—"data, components and systems, expertise in the field, and training for employees in use of the system." Four Japanese companies, including Nissan and Mitsubishi, bought the classified software from Hoffman for undercover payments that totaled over $750,000. He also tried to develop customers in Germany, Italy, Israel, and South Africa. Late in 1989, his secretary at SAIC noticed a fax addressed to Hoffman from Mitsubishi that asked for confirmation that their payment into his account had been received. Adding this to her knowledge of Hoffman's lavish lifestyle, she took her suspicions and a copy of the fax to SAIC's chief counsel. Confronted, Hoffman resigned on the spot and left, but returned to his office during the night when a security video camera captured him carrying out boxes of CONTAM documents. In a joint Customs and Air Force sting operation, investigators posed as South African buyers and documented Hoffman trying to sell them CONTAM modules without an export license. Hoffman was arrested 14 June 1990 and convicted early in 1992 of violations of the Arms Export Control Act and the Comprehensive Anti-Apartheid Act. He was sentenced on 20 April 1992 to 30 months in prison and fined $250,000.

Bosseler, S.J.   *Affidavit,* U.S. District Court, "U.S. v. Ronald Hoffman," 15 June, 1990.
U.S. v. Hoffman   10 F 3d 808 (9th Cir. 1993).
Chicago Tribune   22 Apr 1992, "U.S. Scientist Faces Jail in Sale of Star Wars Software"

HORTON, BRIAN PATRICK, was a US Navy Intelligence Specialist Second Class, assigned to the Nuclear Strike Planning Branch at the Fleet Intelligence Center, Europe and Atlantic, located in Norfolk, Virginia. Between April and October 1982, Horton wrote one letter and made four telephone calls to the Soviet Embassy, offering to provide information on the Single Integrated Operations Plan (SIOP). Based upon evidence accumulated during the investigation, Horton chose to plead guilty under a pretrial agreement which included a posttrial grant of immunity. This allowed the Naval Investigative Service to question Horton after his conviction and sentencing for a period of up to six months to determine any damage to national security caused by his actions. (This technique of posttrial grant-of-immunity encourages the suspect to cooperate in an effort to reduce his sentence.) He was sentenced by a general court-martial on 12 January 1983 to six years' confinement at hard labor, forfeiture of all pay and allowances, a dishonorable discharge, and reduction in pay grade to E-1 for failing to report contacts with the Soviet Embassy in Washington, DC, and for attempting to sell classified information to the USSR. No classified information was actually exchanged and no money was received by Horton. His defense attorney argued that Horton was working on a novel and approached the Soviets to learn their *modus operandi*. The prosecution stated that he had attempted to get between $1,000 and $3,000 for classified information.

Washington Post   14 Jan 1983, "Sailor Sentenced after Bid to Sell Plans to Soviets"
Naval Investigative Service Command, *Espionage*, 1989

HOWARD, EDWARD LEE joined the CIA in 1981. In January 1982 he was assigned to the Soviet/East European Division for training as a case officer in Moscow. He had been given all the data needed to work in Moscow: names of agents, surveillance operations, and the identities of other CIA officers in the Soviet Union. Just as he was about to leave for Moscow in June 1983, he failed his polygraph tests on matters concerning marital relations, petty theft, drinking, and a pattern of past drug use. Asked to resign, he left bewildered and angry. He finally made contact with Soviet officials in Washington, DC, and arranged a meeting in Vienna. He met with KGB officers on three trips to Vienna between 1984 and 1985 and received payment for classified information. Meanwhile, he moved to New Mexico and began working for the New Mexico legislature as a budget analyst. According to news reports, Howard was one of several CIA employees identified by Soviet defector Vitaly Yurchenko as having sold classified information to the KGB. (Yurchenko also identified Ronald Pelton, former NSA employee, who later was arrested for espionage.) Although placed under surveillance by the FBI at his Albuquerque home, Howard, who had been trained by the CIA in surveillance and evasion tactics, eluded spotters and fled the country. He was followed by the FBI as he moved swiftly from country to country, traveling on his credit card and always ahead of the agents. On 7 August 1986, the Soviet news agency *Tass* announced that Howard had been granted political asylum in the USSR. He reportedly revealed to the KGB the identity of a valuable US intelligence source in Moscow. It is also reported that five American diplomats were expelled from the Soviet Union as *personae non gratae* as a result of information provided by Howard. He was the first CIA officer to defect to the USSR. He died in 2002 after falling down the steps of his dacha outside Moscow.

Washington Post   3 Oct 1985, "2 Ex-CIA Agents Sought by FBI as Possible Spies"
Washington Post   5 Oct 1985, "Affidavit Says Ex-CIA Agent Met High-Level KGB Officers"
Washington Post   20 May 1986, "The CIA Agent Who Sold Out"
Washington Post   18 Jul 1986, "5 American Diplomats Caught by KGB"
Newsday   26 Oct 1986, "Why Edward Lee Howard Sold Out for Money and Revenge"
Newsweek   23 May 1988, "The Spy Who Got Away"
NSI Advisory   1 Aug 2002, "CIA Defector Dies"
Minnick. W.L., *Spies and Provocateurs,* 1992

HUMPHREY, RONALD, an employee of the US Information Agency, and **DAVID TRUONG**, a Vietnamese immigrant, were indicted in early 1978. A search of Truong's apartment at the time of his arrest in January uncovered two Top Secret State Department documents. Humphrey had turned over classified cables and documents to Truong who in turn sent them to the North Vietnamese delegation in Paris via a woman who was a Vietnamese double agent working for the FBI. Testimony indicated that Humphrey supplied documents to Truong in order to obtain the release of his common-law wife and her four children from communist Vietnam. Both Humphrey and Truong were convicted on six counts of espionage on 20 May, and on 15 July each received a 15-year sentence.

Washington Post   21 May 1978, "FBI Continues Spy Case Investigation"
Washington Post   24 May 1978, "Cables in Spy Case Larded with Gossip"

ISMAYLOV, VLADIMIR M., senior Soviet military attaché, was arrested on 19 June 1986 at a remote site in Prince George's County, Maryland, after retrieving Secret documents left by a US Air Force officer who was working undercover with counterespionage agents of the AFOSI and the FBI. Until his expulsion for activities incompatible with his diplomatic role, Col. Ismaylov was the highest ranking air force officer at the Soviet Embassy. Ismaylov, apprehended as he buried a milk carton with $41,100 for the US officer, scuffled briefly with FBI agents. According to an FBI spokesman, the Soviet attaché was after information about the Strategic Defense Initiative research program, and data on the cruise missile, stealth bomber, and a hypersonic passenger jet known as the Trans-Atmospheric Vehicle. The operation was run by the GRU. According to the US officer, the Soviets evaluated the USAF officer for nearly a year before asking him to photograph classified documents. All transactions and communications were to be carried out by the use of dead drops at remote locations.

Washington Post   21 Jun 1986, "Soviet Attaché Arrested, Expelled for Receiving Document"

JEFFRIES, RANDY MILES, messenger for a private stenographic firm in Washington, DC, was arrested on 14 December 1985 and charged with attempting to deliver national defense secrets to the Soviet Union. The firm, a cleared contractor facility, had transcribed closed hearings of the House Armed Services Committee. Jeffries allegedly provided Soviet military officials with at least 40 "sample pages" of Secret and Top Secret transcripts from congressional hearings, offering to hand over a complete package of three documents for $5,000. The investigation of Jeffries began after he was observed by US agents entering the Soviet Military Office in Washington. An FBI undercover agent posing as a Soviet representative contacted the messenger at his residence and arranged a meeting later in the day at a local hotel. Jeffries was arrested as he left the meeting. From 1978 to 1980, he was a support employee for the FBI and reportedly held an agency security clearance. In March 1983 he was convicted of possession of heroin and completed a program for rehabilitation from drug abuse in July 1985. Jeffries entered a plea of guilty on 23 January 1986. On 13 March, Jeffries was sentenced by a Federal judge to from three to nine years' imprisonment. As stated by the court at the time of sentencing, it was obvious that poor security practices at the cleared facility were major contributing factors leading to the loss of classified information.

Washington Post   22 Dec 1985, "FBI Agent Says Suspected Spy Offered to Sell Him Document"
Washington Post   24 Dec 1985, "Transcripts Tied to Jeffries Had Strategic Data"
DoD Security Institute, *Security Awareness Bulletin,* No. 2-90, January 1990, "The Case of Randy Miles Jeffries and Acme Reporting"

JENOTT, ERIC O., Army PFC Eric O. Jenott, 20, assigned to duty as a communication switch operator at the 35th Signal Brigade at Ft. Bragg, North Carolina, since 26 June 1996, was charged on 21 August 1996 with espionage, damaging military property, larceny, and unauthorized access to government computer systems. Specifically, Jenott was accused of providing a classified system password to a Chinese national located at Oak Ridge, Tennessee, who returned to China prior to the arrest. According to Jenott, the password was not in fact Secret and charges related to his penetration of defense computer systems stemmed from his attempt to be helpful when he discovered a weakness in an encoded Army computer system. However, he did admit to having been an active hacker for several years and to breaking into Navy, Air Force, and the Defense Secretary's systems before he joined the Army in 1994. While at Ft. Bragg, Jenott demonstrated to his superior officers that he was able to hack into a US Army system that was supposedly secure. On 3 January 1997, a court-martial found Jenott not guilty of espionage, but guilty of lesser offenses in his original charge. He was sentenced to three years in prison, less the six months already served awaiting trial.

Fayetteville Observer-Times   21 Aug 1996, "Army Accuses Fort Bragg Soldier of Computer Espionage"
Chicago Tribune   22 Aug 1996, "GI Hacker Is Charged with Spying."
Raleigh News & Observer   9 Dec 1996, "Court-martial to Begin in Computer Spying Case"

JONES, GENEVA, a secretary with a Top-Secret clearance in the State Department's Bureau of Politico-Military Affairs, was arrested 3 August 1993 and indicted 31August for theft of government property and transmission of defense information to unauthorized persons. FBI agents say she smuggled classified documents for two years to her friend, West African journalist **DOMINIC NTUBE**, indicted at the same time. Jones was carrying classified government documents with her at the time of arrest. Agents who searched Ntube's Washington, DC, apartment after his arrest on 4 August found thousands of classified cables and 39 CIA documents marked Secret, including documents relating to US military operations in Somalia and Iraq. Some of the material apparently made its way to West African magazines, which had been publishing classified State Department cables for several months. Agents indicated they wire-tapped Jones' phone after several classified US documents were found 10 months earlier in the West African command post of Charles Taylor, leader of a violent movement to overthrow the Liberian government. Ntube reportedly faxed 14 documents he received from Jones to the Liberian rebels. The former State Department employee told the FBI she had been giving Ntube classified cables for about 18 months. In a preliminary hearing, the FBI testified that agents watched her on 16 occasions take documents from the department and hide them in newspapers or a grocery bag. During the month she was under surveillance, she allegedly took more than 130 classified documents from her office. On 31 August, Ntube was indicted with Jones for receiving stolen property and for transmitting national defense information to unauthorized persons. In June 1994, Jones pleaded guilty to 21 counts of theft and two counts relating to the unlawful communication of national defense information. In delivering a sentence of 37 months in prison (longer than what the prosecution had asked), US District Judge Harold H. Greene stated, "Somebody would have to be a complete moron not to know that when you work for the State Department you can't take documents out and give them to anybody."

Washington Post	5 Aug 1993, "FBI Arrests Two in Theft of State Dept. Documents"
Washington Post	31 Aug 1993, "Two Indicted in Theft of State Department Documents"

KADISH, BEN-AMI, 84, was arrested 22 April 2008 on four counts. Three were subsequently dropped, and in December 2008 he pleaded guilty to the one: conspiracy to act as an unregistered agent of the government of Israel. Kadish, a mechanical engineer, worked for the US Army's Armament Research, Development, and Engineering Center at the Picatinny Arsenal in Dover, New Jersey, from 1963 until 1990. On numerous occasions from 1980 to 1985, Kadish provided classified documents related to the US military, including some relating to US missile defense systems, to an agent of Israel, Yossi Yagur. Yagur, an Israeli citizen, was consul for science affairs at the Israeli Consulate General in Manhattan between 1980 and 1985. He was also Jonathan Pollard's handler. (Pollard is currently serving a life sentence for espionage on behalf of Israel.) Yagur would provide Kadish with shopping lists of classified documents for Kadish to obtain from the US Army library at Picatinny. The documents—some 50 to 100—concerned nuclear weapons, the F-15 jet program and the Patriot missile system. Kadish stopped passing information to Yagur in 1985 but kept in contact with him over the years via telephone and email and visited him in Israel in 2004. There is no evidence in open sources that Kadish was acting for financial gain; rather, he acted out of a desire to help Israel. Kadish was born in Connecticut and is a US citizen. He grew up in Palestine and served in both the British and American military during World War II. At the time of his arrest he was living with his wife in a retirement community in New Jersey. The FBI arrived on Kadish's doorstep in March 2008 to interview him. The following day, Kadish called Yagur, now also retired and living in Israel, and was instructed by Yagur to deny any involvement. (It is not clear from open sources what prompted the FBI visit to Kadish in 2008, 25 years after his activities for Israel, although it is speculated that there may be a connection between Kadish and the Pollard case and that there may have been a larger Israeli spy ring in the US in the mid-1980s than originally thought.) On 29 May 2009, he eventually was fined $50,000, but not given prison time.

cicentre.com   n.d., "Counterintelligence – Espionage – Spy Case – Kadish, Ben-Ami"
Washington Post   23 Apr 2008, "Ex-Prosecutor: New Arrest Shows Reach of 1980s Spy Ring"
US Attorney, Southern District   30 Dec 2008, "Former U.S. Army Arsenal Employee Pleads Guilty to
     of New York, Press Release   Conspiracy to Act as Unregistered Agent of Israel"
Washington Post   31 Dec 2008, "Retiree Pleads Guilty to Giving U.S. Secrets to Israel in the 1980s"

KAMPILES, WILLIAM, served as a watch officer at the CIA Operations Center from March to November 1977. He was arrested in August 1978 on charges he stole a Top Secret technical manual on the KH-11 ("Big Bird") reconnaissance satellite and later sold it for $3,000 to a Soviet agent in Athens, Greece. According to press reports, the satellite was used to monitor troop movements and missile installations in the Soviet Union. Kampiles had resigned from the CIA in November 1977, disappointed at having been told that he was not qualified for work as a field agent (he fervently wished to join the covert part of CIA operations). Before leaving the agency, he smuggled out of the building a copy of the KH-11 manual. He proceeded to Greece in February 1978 where he contacted a Soviet military attaché. Kampiles was the son of Greek immigrants and had family connections in that country. He claimed to have conned the Russians out of a $3,000 advance for the promise of classified information and on his return to the US bragged to friends about his exploits. About this time the CIA was investigating possible leaks concerning the KH-11, since the Soviets were beginning to take countermeasures against the collection platform. Kampiles' identification as a suspect in part followed receipt of a letter to a CIA employee from Kampiles in which he mentioned frequent meetings with a Soviet official in Athens. He hoped to be rehired by the CIA and admitted during a job interview that he had met with Soviet agents in Athens in what he intended as a disinformation exercise to prove his abilities as a first-rate agent. CIA counterintelligence was concerned by these reports and contacted the FBI, who questioned Kampiles until he confessed the theft of the manual and its sale to the Soviets. The former CIA employee maintained that his objective had been to become a double agent. He was sentenced on 22 December to 40 years in prison.

Washington Post   23 Aug 1978, "CIA 'Big Bird' Satellite Manual Allegedly Sold to Soviets"
New York Times   12 Nov 1978 "Spy Trial Focusing on Security in C.I.A."
New York Times   23 Dec 1978, "Ex-Clerk of C.I.A. Gets 40 Years in Sale of Space Secrets to
                                    Soviets"
Washington Post Magazine   4 Dec 1983, "Spy Rings of One"
 Minnick, W.L., *Spies and Provocateurs,* 1992

KAO, YEN MEN, a Chinese national, residing in Charlotte, North Carolina, was arrested on 3 December 1993, after a six-year investigation into a spy ring that sought secrets on advanced naval weapons and technology. According to an official statement, Kao "and several other Chinese nationals" conspired to illegally procure and export classified and embargoed high-technology military items. Kao was also charged with violating US immigration laws. Targeted for illegal export were the Navy's MK 48 Advanced Capability (ADCAP) Torpedo, two F 404-400 General Electric jet engines used to power the Navy's F/A-18 Hornet fighter, and fire-control radar for the F-16 Falcon jet. Although these systems were not delivered to China, Kao was able to transfer embargoed oscillators used in satellites for which Kao paid an FBI informant $24,000 as part of a sting operation. On 22 December, an immigration judge ordered Yen Men Kao's deportation to Hong Kong for overstaying his visa and for "committing acts of espionage against the United States." A decision was made not to prosecute to avoid offending the Chinese government and to protect counterintelligence sources and methods that might have been disclosed in court. Kao, who reportedly owned two Chinese restaurants in Charlotte, had been under FBI surveillance for several years. During this time he met and received instructions from Chinese intelligence agents who offered him $2 million to obtain US weapons technology. According to one Federal official,

Kao had a gambling problem and lost money supplied by his Chinese handlers. Fearing reprisal from the Chinese as well as the US, he requested deportation to Hong Kong rather than mainland China. Kao left behind his wife, a naturalized US citizen, and two children.

Los Angeles Times	5 Dec 1993, "FBI Arrests Chinese National in Spy Ring Investigation"
Washington Times	22 Dec 1993, "Spy Sting Gets Chinese Man Deported"

KEARN, BRUCE LELAND, a Navy operations specialist assigned as command secret control officer on board the USS *Tuscaloosa*, was arrested in March 1984 and convicted at a general court-martial for dereliction of duty, and willfully delivering, transmitting or communicating classified documents to unauthorized persons. No nation was named as having received any of the classified materials. While absent without leave, Kearn left behind a briefcase which was found to contain 147 classified microfiche (copies of nearly 15,000 pages of Secret documents), seven Confidential crypto publications, and child pornographic photographs and literature. He was sentenced to 18 months based on a plea bargain.

Proceedings, *Naval Review*, 1986, p. 14.

KEYSER, DONALD WILLIS, who submitted his resignation from the State Department in July 2004, was arrested 15 September of the same year, charged with trying to conceal a 2003 trip to Taiwan where he met with two Taiwanese intelligence agents. Fluent in Mandarin, Keyser was an expert on China and had worked in the US Foreign Service since 1972. He had had postings in China and Japan and at the time of his resignation was Principal Deputy Assistant Secretary of State. In that position, he was involved in policy debates that were of concern to Taiwan. Because the US does not have formal relations with Taiwan, American diplomats are not allowed to travel to Taiwan on official business. Yet in August 2003, Keyser traveled to China on business and a few days later flew to Tokyo. From there he flew to Taiwan where he spent three days meeting with a young Taiwanese woman, Isabelle Cheng, at Taiwan's National Security Bureau. To conceal his Taiwan trip, Keyser claimed three days of leave for time purportedly spent in Tokyo. He was arrested on 15 September 2004. It was reported that Keyser had been removing classified documents from the State Department since 1992, and had 3,600 documents in his home, some of which were highly classified. After the arrest, Cheng agreed to cooperate with the FBI and handed over copies of Keyser's emails to her that showed he had shared sensitive information with her, Chang, and that indicated he was having an affair with her. In a 13 December 2005 plea-bargain, Keyser pleaded guilty to keeping numerous classified documents in his home and to concealing his relationship with the Taiwanese intelligence agent. He was scheduled to be sentenced 24 February 2006 but sentencing was repeatedly delayed. Finally, on 22 January 2007, Keyser, by then 63, was sentenced to one year in prison, payment of a $25,000 fine, and three years of supervised release for the unlawful removal of classified material from the State Department and for making false statements to the government.

Washington Post	13 Dec 2005, "Guilty Plea in Classified-Document Case"
New York Sun	14 Jul 2006, "A Novel-Like Tale of Cloak, Dagger Unfolds in Court"
Washington Post	6 Aug 2006, "UPDATE: Alleging Lack of Cooperation, Prosecutors Seek to Voice Plea in Classified-Document Case"
U.S. Department of State (www.state.com)	22 Jan 2007, "Ex-Department of State Official Donald Keyser Sentenced in Classified Info Case"

KIM, ROBERT CHAEGUN, a Navy civilian computer specialist, working at the Office of Naval Intelligence in Suitland, Maryland, was charged on 25 September 1996 with passing classified information to a foreign country. He was arrested outside a diplomatic reception at Ft. Myer, Virginia, on 24 September as he stood beside Capt. Baek Dong-Il, a Korean Embassy naval attaché and the alleged recipient of the classified materials. Kim, a native of Korea, became a US citizen in 1974 and had lived in the United States for 30 years. He had access to classified information since 1979. According to investigators, over a five-month period, he passed dozens of classified documents (including some that were Top Secret) out of loyalty to his country of birth. An FBI affidavit states that Kim searched naval computer systems, made copies of sensitive classified intelligence reports, removed classified markings, printed them off, and mailed or passed them in manila envelopes to Baek. The documents included military assessments about North Korea and China and US intelligence assessments of South Korean government officials. In his official capacity, Kim operated a computer program that tracked global shipping movements. However, he had access to highly classified documents from other intelligence agencies. Kim came under surveillance by the Naval Investigative Service when it learned of his contact with Baek. A court-approved search of Kim's office produced a list of classified documents he had illegally passed to the naval attaché. More than 40 documents sent to Baek were intercepted in the mail. Capt. Baek Dong-Il, who enjoyed diplomatic immunity, was subsequently recalled by his government. While there is no evidence that Kim received any payment for his illegal activities, according to one news source, he had requested assistance from the South Koreans in his efforts to find employment with a South Korean intelligence or customs agency after his retirement from his US Navy job. It is also reported that Kim had accumulated a credit card debt of approximately $100,000. On 7 May 1997, Kim pleaded guilty to one count of conspiracy to commit espionage. On 11 July he was sentenced to nine years in prison.

Washington Post	26 Sep 1996, "Navy Worker Is Accused Of Passing Secret; Papers Allegedly Went To S. Korean Officer"
Washington Post	2 Oct 1996, "Kim Allegedly Sought Job With S. Korea"
Los Angeles Times	8 May 1997, "Ex-Analyst Admits Spying For S. Korea In Plea Bargain"

KING, DONALD WAYNE, Navy Airman and **RONALD DEAN GRAF**, Navy Airman Apprentice, both assigned to the Naval Air Station in Belle Chasse, Louisiana, pleaded guilty to conspiracy to commit espionage and larceny of government property following their apprehension by special agents of the Naval Investigative Service. The pair were apprehended by the NIS at a motel in New Orleans after they delivered $150,000 worth of sensitive and classified aircraft parts and technical manuals to an undercover NIS agent they believed was a foreign government representative. The stolen government property and manuals (about 30 items in total) dealt with technology pertaining to the Navy's P-3 anti-submarine aircraft. The investigation was initiated in January 1989, after an informant notified the New Orleans NIS office that King and Graf were trying to sell aircraft parts they had stolen from the Naval Station at Belle Chasse. The airmen were also charged with the sale of cocaine. King was sentenced to 10 years, reduction in rank to E-1, forfeiture of all pay and a dishonorable discharge. Graft was sentenced to five years, reduction in rank to E-1, forfeiture of all pay and a dishonorable discharge. Their motivation for espionage is not known; however, Graf is quoted as claiming that he did it to pay off debts amounting to $1,000.

| *New Orleans Times-Picayune* | 5 Mar 1989, "2 Navy Clerks Accused of Spying" |
| *New Orleans Times-Picayune* | 7 Jul 1989, "Jail Terms Given in Spy Case" |

Case summary provided by Albert E. DiFerderico, US Naval Criminal Investigative Service

KOECHER, KARL FRANTISEK, a former CIA employee, and his wife, were arrested 27 November 1984 as they were preparing to fly to Switzerland. At the time, he was believed to be the first foreign agent to have penetrated the CIA, having operated successfully as an "illegal" for Czech intelligence for 19 years. In 1962 Koecher was trained as a foreign agent by Czech intelligence. He and his wife staged a phony defection to the US in 1965 and soon became known as an outspoken anti-Communist member of the academic community in New York City. Both became naturalized citizens in 1971 and Koecher obtained a translator job with the CIA two years later where he translated Top Secret materials until 1975. Koecher, who claimed that he was a double agent, was arrested after being observed making frequent contact with KGB operatives. According to Federal prosecutors, Mrs. Koecher operated as a paid courier for Czech intelligence until 1983. An FBI agent testified that from February 1973 to August 1983, Karl Koecher passed on to Czech agents highly classified materials including names of CIA personnel. However, the case never came to trial. On 11 February 1985, Koecher was exchanged in Berlin for Soviet dissident Anatoly Shcharansky. The Koechers' motivation was primarily loyalty to their country, but also included the prospect of money and perhaps even the thrill of being double agents.

New York Times	28 Nov 1984, "Man Charged with Passing State Secrets"
New York Times	5 Dec 1984, "Wife is Held in Contempt of Court for Refusing to Testify "
New York Times	13 Jan 1985, "Intrigue and Countercharges Mark Case of Purported Spies"
Washington Post	17 Apr 1988, "Moscow Mole in the CIA"

KOSTADINOV, PENYU B., a commercial counselor at the Bulgarian Commercial Office in New York, was arrested in December 1983 at a New York restaurant as he exchanged a sum of money for classified material. Kostadinov had attempted to recruit a graduate student who had access to documents related to nuclear energy. The unnamed American agreed to work under FBI control to apprehend the agent. One of Kostadinov's official functions was to arrange for exchange students between Bulgaria and the US. Although Kostadinov claimed diplomatic immunity at the time of his arrest, this was later denied by a Federal court. In June 1985, Kostadinov was swapped along with three other Soviet Bloc agents for 25 persons who had "been helpful" to the US.

New York Times	24 Sep 1983, "Bulgarian Charged as Spy"
Washington Post	25 Sep 1983, "Bulgarian Man Arraigned"

KOTA, SUBRAHMANYAM, and **ALURU J. PRASAD**. On 8 October 1995, Indian businessman, Aluru J. Prasad, and 10 days later, software engineer Subrahmanyan Kota, were arrested and detained for their involvement in a spy ring that sold highly sensitive defense technology to the KGB between 1985 and 1990. Prasad, a wealthy Indian national who frequently visited the US, was alleged to have been an agent of the KGB. Kota, a naturalized US citizen, was president of the Boston Group computer consulting firm. According to an FBI affidavit, the pair met Russian agents in Bermuda, Portugal, Switzerland, and other foreign locations and at these meetings passed classified defense information. At the time of their indictment, it was revealed that Kota and another conspirator, Vemuri Reddy, had been arrested the previous December by FBI agents who were posing as Russian intelligence agents, to whom they had attempted to sell (for $300,000) micro-organisms used in the production of a high-tech drug. Beginning in 1989, Prasad plotted with Kota of Northborough, Massachusetts, and other unnamed persons to obtain classified technology from a network defense contractor employee. Prasad and Kota specifically sought information about mercury cadmium telluride missile detectors, radar-absorbing coating used on stealth fighters and bombers, and semiconductor components used in infrared missile-tracking systems. According to their indictment, the two received $100,000 for information about each project. On 29 October 1996, former KGB intelligence officer Vladimir Galkin was arrested as he attempted to enter the US at Kennedy Airport in New York. Galkin was alleged to have been Kota and Prasad's contact with the

KGB and met with Kota in Cyprus beginning in late 1990. Although Galkin had not committed espionage on American soil, he was charged for his involvement in the conspiracy. In June 1996, under a plea agreement, Kota pleaded guilty to selling stolen biotech material and evasion of income taxes and agreed to testify against Prasad. He admitted that he was paid a total of $95,000 by Prasad and his alleged KGB colleagues. Prasad's first trial ended in a mistrial; however, in a second trial in December 1996 he was convicted of espionage charges. Under a plea agreement Prasad was sentenced to the 15 months he had served awaiting his trial and agreed to return to India. On 13 November, accused KGB intelligence agent Vladimir Galkin was released.

Boston Globe   19 Oct 1995, "Northborough Man Charged With Espionage"
Boston Globe   12 Jun 1996, "A Post-Cold War Spy Story Comes to Life"
Washington Times   5 Nov 1996, Computer Check of Visa at Airport IDs Spy Suspect"

KUNKLE, CRAIG DEE, former Chief Petty Officer who specialized in antisubmarine warfare, was arrested on 10 January 1989 as he attempted to sell classified information for $5,000 to FBI agents posing as Soviet diplomats. The arrest took place at a Williamsburg, Virginia, motel. On 9 December Kunkle mailed a packet of diagrams, photographs and information related to antisubmarine warfare tactics to an Alexandria, Virginia, post office box he believed to be a Soviet drop point. The material was collected by Federal agents who had been in communication with Kunkle on six previous occasions. An investigation by the Naval Investigative Service and FBI began in early December 1988 when Kunkle's attempt to contact the Soviet Embassy in Washington was intercepted. Kunkle had served for 12 years in the Navy in antisubmarine squadrons in the Atlantic and Pacific fleets and was discharged in 1985 under less than honorable conditions, reportedly for multiple incidents including indecent exposure. Kunkle also had a history of alcohol and drug abuse in addition to marital and financial problems. During his period of active duty, he held a Secret clearance. The former Chief Petty Officer had since been employed as a security guard at a local hospital. At the time of arrest Kunkle stated that he offered to sell classified information because he was short of cash and angry with the Navy. Kunkle was indicted on one count of attempted espionage and ordered held without bond. He pleaded not guilty to the charge. On 4 May 1989 Kunkle changed his plea to guilty because, he said, he did not want to subject his family to a trial. He had faced a maximum sentence of life in prison and a $250,000 fine. The judge imposed a 12-year sentence (agreed upon by prosecutors and Kunkle's attorneys) and, noting Kunkle's money problems, fined him $550. He was not eligible for parole and was placed on three years' probation in addition to the sentence.

New York Times   11 Jan 1989, "Former Navy Man Is Charged As a Spy"
New York Times   19 Jan 1989, "Ex-Navyman Denies Trying to Sell Secrets"

KUO, TAI SHEN, 58, a naturalized US citizen born in Taiwan, imported furniture from China and had a store in New Orleans at the time of his arrest on 11 February 2008 for spying for the People's Republic of China (PRC). A member of a prominent Taiwanese family, Kuo had immigrated to the US in 1972, attending college in Louisiana before building his own business in New Orleans, primarily involving furniture. He maintained an office in Beijing and took steps towards establishing two companies in the US to pursue contracts related to the US sale of defense technology to Taiwan. Masquerading as a Taiwanese agent when in fact he was working for the Beijing government, Kuo cultivated a relationship with **GREGG WILLIAM BERGERSEN**, a 51-year-old Pentagon weapons systems policy analyst in the Defense Security Cooperation Agency, the agency that implements DoD's foreign military sales program. From Bergersen Kuo obtained sensitive and classified national defense information regarding US military sales to Taiwan. The period of espionage was March 2007 until February 2008. An unidentified Chinese agent (referred to in the government's affidavit as "PRC Official A") gave Kuo instructions on what information and documents to collect. Kuo is believed to have received $50,000 from PRC Official A, who had lured Kuo into espionage with promises of helping him secure business deals in China. In turn, Kuo gave thousands of dollars in gambling money and trips to Las Vegas to Bergersen, who provided Kuo with the requested information. Bergersen passed classified documents to Kuo, believing that the information was to be given to Taiwan, an American ally, and also that Kuo would eventually give him a post-retirement job in Kuo's future defense consulting firm. A third person in the ring was **YU XIN KANG**, 33, a Chinese national resident alien who had met Kuo in Beijing years earlier and by 2007 was an employee in Kuo's New Orleans furniture company. Kang periodically acted as a go-between for Kuo and PRC Official A, carrying documents to Beijing where she had an apartment. Kuo was sentenced on 8 August 2008 to nearly 16 years in prison for being an unregistered agent of the PRC. Bergersen pleaded guilty in April 2008 and agreed to help federal authorities build their case against his co-conspirators; on 11 July 2008 he was given a 57-month sentence, plus three years' supervised release. Kang was sentenced on 1 August 2008 to 18 months and three years of supervised release for aiding and abetting an unregistered agent of the PRC. In May 2009 another individual, a former Air Force Lieutenant Colonel, was charged with giving classified data to China via Kuo; he has pleaded not guilty.

Times-Picayune	1 Apr 2008, "Arms Analyst Admits Role in Spy Ring"
New York Times	10 Jul 2008, "Spy Cases Raise Concern on China's Intentions"
Department of Justice, Press Release	1 Aug 2008, "New Orleans Woman Sentenced to Prison for Aiding and Abetting Unregistered Agent of China"
New York Times	8 Aug 2008, "US Man Who Spied for China Gets Nearly 16 Years"

LALAS, STEVEN JOHN, a former State Department communications officer stationed with the embassy in Athens, was arrested in Northern Virginia on 3 May 1993 and charged with passing sensitive military information to Greek officials. Although Lalas originally claimed that he had been recruited by a Greek military official in 1991 and feared for the welfare of relatives living in Greece were he not to cooperate, authorities later stated that he began spying for the Greek government in 1977 when he was with the US Army. It is estimated that he passed 700 highly classified documents, including papers dealing with plans and readiness for US military strategy in the Balkans and a US assessment of Greece's intentions toward the former Yugoslavia. Athens was Lalas' fourth communications posting with the State Department. He had previously served in Belgrade, Istanbul, and in Taiwan. During his espionage career he earned a steady income stealing, then selling, DIA reports about troop strength, political analyses and military discussions contained in cables between the US Embassy in Athens and the White House, FBI communications about counterterrorism efforts, and the names and job descriptions of CIA agents stationed overseas. Greek handlers allegedly paid him $20,000 to provide about 240 documents from 1991 to 1993. The government first learned of the espionage activities in February 1993, when an official of the Greek Embassy in Washington made a statement to a State Department officer indicating that he knew the contents of a Secret communication from the US Embassy in Athens to the State Department. Lalas was later identified (through a video monitoring system) stealing documents intended for destruction. In June 1993 Lalas pleaded guilty to one count of conspiracy to commit espionage and on 16 September was sentenced to 14 years in Federal prison without possibility of parole. Prosecutors had recommended the 14-year sentence in return for Lalas' promise to reveal what documents he turned over and to whom. The full extent of his espionage activity was revealed prior to sentencing only after he failed two FBI polygraph examinations. Lalas is of Greek descent, but was born in the US.

Washington Post	4 May 1993, "Va. Arrest Made in a Spy Case From Greece"
New York Times	4 May 1993, "Am. Employee at Embassy in Athens Arrested as Possible Spy"
New York Times	6 May 1993, "US Embassy Employee Sold Secrets to Greeks, F.B.I. Says"
Washington Post	16 Sep 1993, "A 14-Year Sentence for Selling Secrets"

LEE, PETER H., a nuclear physicist who worked at key research facilities for more than 30 years, turned himself in to authorities and pleaded guilty on 8 December 1997 to two felony counts, one for passing national defense information and the other for providing false statements to the government. Dr. Lee admitted that in 1985, while working as a research physicist at Los Alamos National Laboratory, he traveled to the People's Republic of China. During this visit Lee discussed with a group of approximately 30 Chinese scientists the construction of hohlraums, diagnostic devices used in conjunction with lasers to create microscopic nuclear detonations. Prosecutors stated Lee acknowledged that he knew the information was classified. The second charge against Lee concerned disclosures he failed to make in 1997 while he was working on classified research projects for TRW. Before he traveled to China on vacation, Lee was required to fill out a security form in which he stated he would not be giving lectures on his work. Upon his return, he had to fill out a second form in which he confirmed that he did not give any lectures of a technical nature. However, as Lee later confessed to the FBI, he lied on both forms because he intended to and did, in fact, deliver lectures to Chinese scientists that discussed his work on microwave backscattering from the sea surface. Dr. Lee told the FBI that he disclosed the information because he wanted to help his Chinese counterparts and he wanted to enhance his reputation in China. According to US government sources, Lee did receive compensation for the information he provided to the Chinese in the form of travel and hotel accommodations. The case resulted from an investigation by agents from the FBI's Foreign Counterintelligence Squad. On 26 March 1998, Dr. Lee was sentenced to one year in a community corrections facility, three years' probation, and ordered to perform 3,000 hours of community service and pay $20,000 in fines.

Los Angeles Times   9 Dec 1997, "Physicist Admits Passing Laser Secrets to Chinese Scientists"
Washington Post   12 Dec 1997, "Taiwan Born Scientist Passes Defense Information"
Counterintelligence   Mar 1998, "US Physicist Pleads Guilty"
  News Digest

LEONOV, YURIY P., a lieutenant colonel in Soviet military intelligence (GRU), fronting as a Soviet air force attaché, was apprehended on 18 August 1983 after receiving 60 pounds of government documents from an editor working under FBI control. The following day Leonov, who had diplomatic immunity, was declared *persona non grata* and expelled from the country. This ended a two-year recruitment attempt by Leonov against Armand B. Weiss, an editor of technical publications and former government consultant. Weiss had previously held a Top Secret clearance. In all, Leonov paid Weiss $1,800 for sensitive but unclassified publications on weapon systems. Ultimately, Leonov demanded a classified document. Under FBI direction, Weiss provided the item with a large number of highly technical publications for $500 cash. Leonov was arrested by agents waiting outside the office.

Washington Post   16 Sep 1983, "Soviet Military Spy Caught in FBI Trap"

LESSENTHIEN, KURT G., a Navy petty officer, arrested in Orlando, Florida, on 3 April 1996, was charged with attempted espionage after offering information about nuclear submarine technology to a Russian government representative. Lessenthien was subsequently contacted by undercover agents of the FBI and Naval Criminal Investigative Service posing as Russian agents. At the time Lessenthien was an instructor at the Navy Nuclear Power School in Orlando and was very knowledgeable about the design and operation of submarine motors. It was reported that the petty officer, in a phone call to the Russian Embassy, offered Top Secret information about the movement of US submarines in exchange for thousands of dollars. According to one media source, Lessenthien accumulated nearly $25,000 in credit card debt on a "relentless pursuit of women" that he intended to marry. A Navy psychiatrist testified that he suffered personality flaws that drove him to ruin an excellent military record. However, a Navy prosecutor stated that Lessenthien decided to become a spy for money and excitement, not love, and that the petty officer had been storing classified materials since 1991. On 28 October, Lessenthien was sentenced by a military court to life imprisonment, but will serve 27 years under a plea agreement. He was also given a dishonorable discharge and ordered to forfeit all pay and benefits.

Washington Post	4 Apr 1996, "Petty Officer Arrested on Spy Charges"
Orlando Sentinel	24 Apr 1996, "Orlando Sailor in Spy Arrest."
Virginian-Pilot (Norfolk)	29 Oct 1996, "Lessenthien Gets 27 Years in Espionage Case"

LIPKA, ROBERT STEPHAN, former National Security Agency staff member, was taken into custody on 23 February 1996 at his home in Millersville, Pennsylvania, and charged with committing espionage while working as a communications clerk from 1964 to 1967. An Army enlisted man between the age of 19 and 22, Lipka worked in the NSA central communications room and reportedly provided the KGB with a constant stream of highly classified reports. He is believed to have caused extensive damage to US intelligence collection activities. According to James Bamford, writing in the *Los Angeles Times*, since Lipka provided Top Secret information to the KGB during the war in Vietnam, he may have been responsible for the loss of American lives. He is said to have used dead drops along the C&O Canal near the Potomac River in Washington and was paid between $500 and $1000 per delivery. Lipka left NSA in 1967 and stopped meeting with his KGB handlers in 1974. He became a suspect in 1993 as a result of information believed to have been provided to the FBI by his ex-wife. His role in espionage was confirmed by FBI agents posing as Russian contacts. According to an FBI spokesman, while the government was aware of a major security breach in the 1960s, it had not been able to identify Lipka as a suspect until it had received the additional information. It is believed that Lipka is the young soldier described in the autobiography of former KGB major general Kalugin who tells of a walk-in in the mid-1960s who was interested in money. According to Kalugin, the documents that the soldier passed included Top Secret NSA reports to the White House and copies of communications on US troop movements around the world. The price reportedly paid by the Soviets during the period of his betrayal was $27,000. On 23 May 1997, Lipka pleaded guilty to one count of espionage in exchange for a jail term of no more than 18 years. On 24 September, he was sentenced to serve a term of 18 years in Federal prison.

Washington Post	24 Feb 1996, "FBI Arrests Ex-Soldier as Mysterious KGB Spy in Supersecret NSA"
Los Angeles Times	3 Mar 1996, "Has a 30-year Mystery Unraveled?"
Wall Street Journal	21 Nov 1996, "How the FBI Broke Spy Case That Baffled Agency for 30 Years"
Baltimore Sun	24 May 1997, "Ex-clerk at NSA Is Guilty of Spying; Former Soldier Sold Secret Documents to Soviets in Mid-1960s"

LONETREE, CLAYTON JOHN, Marine Corps security guard at the US Embassy in Moscow from September 1984 to March 1986, and later in Vienna, was placed under detention on 31 December 1986 after he acknowledged his involvement with a female KGB officer, Violette Seina, who had previously been a telephone operator and translator at the US Embassy in Moscow. Soon after their relationship began, Seina introduced Lonetree to her "Uncle Sasha" who was later identified by US intelligence as being a KGB agent. It was alleged at the time that Sgt. Lonetree had a sexual liaison with Seina, and had in fact allowed Soviet agents after-hours access to the US Embassy. In December 1986, Lonetree turned himself in to authorities at the US Embassy in Vienna, Austria, where he was stationed. Also arrested and charged with collaboration with Lonetree was Corporal Arnold Bracy who was also alleged to have been romantically involved with Soviet women. As the investigation proceeded, five other Marine guards were detained on suspicion of espionage, lying to investigators, or for improper fraternization with foreign nationals. Lonetree was tried on 13 counts including espionage. Among these counts were charges that he conspired with Soviet agents to gather names and photographs of American intelligence agents, to provide personality data on American intelligence agents, and to provide information concerning the floor plans of the US Embassies in Moscow and Vienna. On 21 August 1987 Lonetree was convicted of espionage and 12 related counts by a military court. Three days later he was sentenced to 30 years' imprisonment, fined $5,000, loss of all pay and allowances, reduced to the rank of private, and given a dishonorable discharge. Espionage charges against Bracy and all of the other Marines have since been dropped. According to reports in late 1987, intensive investigations have led to the conclusion that the former guards did not, as earlier believed, allow Soviet agents to penetrate the US Embassy in Moscow. In May, 1988, Lonetree's sentence was reduced to 25 years, in 1992 to 20 years, and later to 15 years. In February 1996 he was released.

Washington Post	10 Feb 1987, "'Success Story' Marine May Face Trial for His Life"
Washington Post	30 Jul 1987, "Envoy Blamed for Lax Security"
Washington Post	17 Jan 1988, "Spy Scandal Snowballed, Melted Away"
Richmond Times-Dispatch	25 Feb 1996, "Lonetree May Find Stigma Lives On"

Naval Investigative Service Command, *Espionage*, 1989

MADSEN, LEE EUGENE, a Navy Yeoman assigned to the Strategic Warning Staff at the Pentagon, was arrested 14 August 1979 for selling classified material to an FBI undercover agent for $700. None of 22 highly classified documents taken by Madsen is known to have fallen into the hands of foreign agents; however, it is believed that he had intended to sell them to organized crime figures dealing in narcotics. Madsen, a homosexual, is quoted as saying that he stole Top Secret documents "to prove...I could be a man and still be gay." On 26 October 1979 he was sentenced to eight years in prison.

Washington Post	27 Oct 1979, "Sailor Receives 8 Years in Jail"

MAK, CHI, 68 at the time of sentencing and a former employee of Anaheim-based Power Paragon, Inc., was arrested on 28 October 2005. Mak, along with his wife (Rebecca Chiu), brother (Tai Mak), sister-in-law (Fuk Li) and nephew (Billy), was charged with conspiring to steal sensitive military information as well as failing to register as an agent of a foreign government. As a lead project engineer at Power Paragon, a defense contractor, Mak aided the US Navy with its research project on a Quiet Electric Drive (QED) propulsion system that would reduce a vessel's sound signature. Mak was born in China in 1940 and moved to the US in 1978. He and his wife became citizens in 1985 and lived in a Los Angeles suburb. Mak held a steady job where he was regularly promoted and rewarded. His job gave him access to sensitive plans for Navy ships, submarines, and weapons, including details of the electrical power system in Virginia-class submarines that, if provided to the Chinese, would allow them to track the submarines. The five defendants were accused specifically of transferring data onto three encrypted disks that Tai Mak and Fuk Li attempted to transport to China in October 2005. One piece of evidence against the group was a to-do list of intelligence targets, written in Chinese and said to be instructions from Beijing on the kinds of technology Mak should try to acquire. While not all the materials sent to China over time may have been formally classified, Mak's conspiracy to pass them constituted a violation of US export control laws. Mak was arrested in Los Angeles after FBI agents stopped his brother and sister-in-law as they boarded a flight to China. The disks they carried contained information on a submarine propulsion system, a solid-state power switch for ships, and a PowerPoint presentation on the future of power electronics. Mak was convicted on 11 May 2007 of conspiracy to violate export control laws and failing to register as a foreign agent. He was sentenced on 25 March 2008 to 24½ years in prison and fined $50,000. His wife was sentenced to three years (plus an agreement to renounce her US citizenship and return to China on her release); Mak's brother Tai Mak received a 10-year sentence, Tai's wife three years' probation, and son

Billy, 11 months (time already served in custody). Tai Mak and his family are not American citizens and will be deported after completing their sentences.

Washington Post	6 Jun 2007, "Plea Deal Ends China Tech Export Case"
Los Angeles Times	7 June 2007, "5th Defendant in Spy Case Pleads Guilty"
Washington Times	25 Mar 2008, "Spy for China Gets 24 Years"
Los Angeles Times	22 Apr 2008, "Man Gets 10 Years in China Spy Case"
Los Angeles Times	3 Oct 2008, "3-Year Sentence in China Spy Case"

MAYNARD, JOHN RAYMOND, Navy Seaman, while on unauthorized absence, was found to have 51 Top Secret documents in his personal locker. Until the time of his arrest in August 1983, Maynard was assigned to the staff of the Commander in Chief Pacific Fleet in Hawaii as an intelligence specialist. He was convicted at a general court-martial for wrongfully removing classified material and was sentenced to 10 years' confinement. Maynard's sentence was later reduced to three years.

MAZIARZ, GARY, 37, a reserve gunnery sergeant in the Marine Corps, was arrested October 2006, accused of being part of a theft ring at Camp Pendleton, California. Documents stolen included classified computer files on potential terrorists that Mariarz shared with military reserve officers who worked with anti-terrorism units of police departments in Los Angeles County. One of the officers was a Marine reserve colonel and detective with the Los Angeles sheriff's department, a counterterrorism specialist and allegedly the instigator of the enterprise; he was also the founder of the Los Angeles Terrorism Early Warning Group, a task force of law enforcement agencies. Maziarz pleaded guilty in July 2007 to mishandling more than 100 classified documents. He also named three senior reserve officers at Camp Pendleton, along with two sergeants who were charged in June 2008. The officers are still under investigation. There was no indication that any information had been passed to foreign agents. Mariarz claimed at his court-martial he knew his group was violating security regulations. But he said that he had acted out of patriotism in attempting to break down the bureaucratic walls between military and civilian agencies that he felt were hampering intelligence sharing and coordination and thus making the nation more vulnerable to terrorists. Indeed, transferring classified information to uncleared persons, even if they were employed by US agencies, was a clear violation of security rules. In July 2007 Mariarz was convicted. In a plea agreement he agreed, in exchange for a short 26-month prison sentence, to testify against his alleged co-conspirators and not to speak with the media. In November 2008, he broke his agreement by telling the *San Diego Union-Tribune* that "dozens of files" that were passed were dossiers on Muslims and Arabs living in Southern California. The FBI denies it monitors such groups. It was purely by chance that the theft ring was exposed. In October 2006 a colonel at Camp Pendleton reported to Navy special agents that trophy weapons, brought from Iraq by the Marines, were missing. An internal investigation focused on Maziarz, who had worked in Iraq. He had stockpiled the stolen goods in his apartment and in storage units in California and Virginia. Since investigators not only found stashes of Iraqi weapons and war memorabilia, but also classified documents, the investigation broadened to include espionage.

Washington Post	5 Jan 2007, "Theft Probe Leads to N. Va. Storage Site"
Secrecy News	12 Oct 2007, "Information Sharing, by Hook or by Crook"
San Diego Union-Tribune	18 Jul 2008, "2 Marines Charged in Secrets Theft Ring"
San Diego Union-Tribune	17 Nov 2008, "Former Marine Outlines Secret Dossiers; Muslims, Arabs Not Targeted, FBI Says"

MEHALBA, AHMED FATHY, a naturalized American of Egyptian descent, was arrested on 29 September 2003 at Boston's Logan International Airport after arriving from Cairo. He had taken emergency leave from his job at Guantanamo Bay with the Titan Corporation to visit his father in Egypt. (Titan is the defense contractor that supplies translators for Army interrogators at Guantanamo.) On his return, in a routine examination by Customs and Border Protection officers, he was found to have 132 computer disks in his baggage, one of which contained hundreds of separate documents labeled "Secret," or "Secret/Noforn." He was charged with making false statements to federal agents, since he repeatedly denied that he had any classified information from Guantanamo in his possession. He was indicted in November 2003 on charges of improperly gathering military information and lying to the FBI to which he pleaded not guilty. Born in Alexandria, Egypt, Mehalba immigrated to Salem, Massachusetts, in the early 1990s. He filed for bankruptcy in 1997, owing creditors $27,000. In 2000 he joined the US Army, twice failed to pass an interrogator course at Fort Huachuca, and was discharged for medical reasons (obesity) in 2001. Despite his discharge and bankruptcy, he was able to get a job in 2003 with Titan and was granted a security clearance by the Army. The government could not prove that he had shared classified information with anyone while abroad. In January 2005, Mehalba agreed to plead guilty under an agreement with prosecutors. He was sentenced 18 February 2005 to 20 months in prison. With good behavior and time already served, he was released in 22 days. The light sentence reflected the judge's opinion that Mehalba was suffering from untreated bipolar disorder and depression when he took the documents. The judge said, "I really do believe the agreed-upon sentence reflects a measured, well-calibrated and in fact humane disposition." The case illustrates some of the vetting problems involved with hiring native-speaking linguists, so urgently needed in Iraq.

New York Times	30 Sep 2003, "Guantanamo Bay Aide is Arrested at Boston Airport"
Boston Globe	1 Oct 2003, "Guantanamo Translator Seized at Logan"
New York Times	1 Oct 2003, "Guantanamo Inquiry Widens as Civilian Translator is Held"
Boston Globe	8 Jan 2005, "Plea Deal Signals Trouble with Case Against Translator"
Boston Globe	19 Feb 2005, "Translator Sentenced in Guantanamo Documents Case"

MICHELSON, ALICE, an East German national, was apprehended 1 October 1984 as she was boarding a flight in New York to Czechoslovakia with tape recordings hidden in a cigarette pack. Michelson, apparently acting as courier for Soviet intelligence, had been given the classified material by a US Army sergeant who was posing as a KGB collaborator. Michelson was indicted and held without bail; however, before coming to trial she was exchanged (June 1985), along with three other Soviet Bloc agents, for 25 persons who had "been helpful" to the US. The FBI has described the case as "a classic spy operation."

Washington Post	3 Oct 1984, "East German Woman Charged with Spying"
Washington Post	3 Oct 1984, "FBI Agent, German, Analyst in Intelligence Cases"
New York Times	11 Oct 1984, "East German Indicted in Spy Plot"

MILLER, RICHARD W., first member of the FBI to be indicted for espionage, was arrested with two accomplices, **SVETLANA** and **NIKOLAI OGORODNIKOV**, on 3 October 1984. According to news reports, Miller provided classified documents to the Ogorodnikovs, two pro-Soviet Russian émigrés, and demanded $50,000 in gold and $15,000 cash in return. Miller, who was faced with financial difficulties, is alleged to have been sexually involved with Svetlana Ogorodnikov and was preparing to travel with her to Vienna at the time of his arrest. A search of Miller's residence uncovered several classified documents. At the time of their trial the Ogorodnikovs were accused of having been "utility agents" for the KGB since 1980. After a 10-week trial, and in an agreement with Federal prosecutors, each pleaded guilty to one count of conspiracy. Nikolai Ogorodnikov was immediately sentenced to eight years imprisonment. His wife later received a sentence of 18 years. Miller pleaded innocent and after 11 weeks of testimony, a mistrial was declared. Following a second trial which ended on 19 June 1986, Miller was found guilty of espionage and bribery. His claim that he was trying to infiltrate the KGB as a double agent was rejected by the jury. On 14 July 1986, Miller was sentenced to two consecutive life terms and 50 years on other charges. This conviction following his second trial was overturned in 1989 on the grounds that US District Judge David Kenyon erred in admitting polygraph evidence. Miller was granted bail in October 1989 while awaiting a new trial on charges that he passed Top Secret FBI data to the Soviet woman who was his lover. Miller was forbidden to leave the Los Angeles area without special permission and underwent therapy as ordered by the Probation Department. On October 9, 1990, he was convicted on all counts of espionage for the second time and, on 4 February 1991, was sentenced to 20 years in Federal prison. On 28 January 1993, a Federal Appeals Court upheld his conviction. On 6 May 1994, Miller was released from prison following the reduction of his sentence to 13 years by a Federal judge.

Washington Post	4 Oct 1984, "FBI Agent Charged in Espionage"
Washington Post	5 Oct 1984, "Accused Spies Portrayed as Incompetents"
Time Magazine	15 Oct 1984, "Spy vs. Spy Saga"
Los Angeles Times	5 Feb 1991, "Miller Gets 20-Year Term for Spying"

MIRA, FRANCISCO DE ASSIS, an Air Force computer specialist stationed in Germany, was charged in April 1983 with providing classified defense information to East Germany. Mira, a naturalized American born in Spain, and two West German accomplices sold information on American codes and radar to the East German State Security Service. In August 1982, while assigned to duties at a US air base at Birkenfeld, West Germany, Mira photographed the cover and random pages of code books and maintenance schedules of air defense radar installations. He processed the photos, with the help of his girlfriend, and asked two local minor drug dealers to carry the material to East Germany and attempt to make contact with the KGB. They made several trips between September 1982 and March 1983, each time passing information provided by Mira, and were paid between $1,136 and $1,515 per visit. Realizing he was in over his head and feeling used by his accomplices, Mira sought to extricate himself from a bad situation. In March 1983, Mira went to the AFOSI and related what he had done, not realizing how thorough the investigative process would be. Under questioning, Mira claimed that he wanted to become a double agent and that he "wanted to show the Air Force I could do more with my intelligence." But in subsequent interviews he admitted he had originated the idea to commit espionage to make some money, and enlisted the two West Germans to assist him. He was disgruntled because he had not gotten the assignment he had wanted. In August 1984 Mira was dishonorably discharged and sentenced to 10 years' confinement. Under a plea bargain he served only seven years of the sentence.

Stars and Stripes	29 Aug 1984, "Airman is Sentenced for Spy Activities"

MONTAPERTO, RONALD N., a former DIA intelligence analyst, in late 2003 admitted to FBI and Navy counterintelligence agents that he had verbally provided Secret and Top Secret information to Chinese intelligence officers over several years (1989 to 2001). Back in 1982 Dr. Montaperto had been one of six DIA analysts selected to participate in a CIA-sponsored pilot program to foster social and professional interactions between DIA's China experts and the Chinese military. After the program ended, Montaperto continued to maintain those close relationships as part of his official duties but did not always report these meetings to DIA, a violation of security rules. Montaperto began work for the DIA in 1981 as an intelligence analyst and went on in 1992 to become a research professor at the National Defense University. He later was dean of academics at the US Pacific Command's Asia Pacific Center for Security Studies until early 2004 when he was dismissed. Montaperto was first investigated by the FBI in the late 1980s after a Chinese defector told US intelligence that Beijing had developed a handful of clandestine sources, "dear friends" to China. The FBI suspected Montaperto but later cleared him. Then in early 1991, when the FBI was again interviewing him, he admitted to having verbally provided contacts with information but could not recall the specifics. Nor was the FBI itself able to identify the precise nature of classified information that Montaperto had passed. The case was dropped for lack of evidence. In August 2001 the FBI and Navy, still in pursuit, initiated a "ruse" operation against Montaperto offering him work on a China-related project, but this would involve his taking a CI polygraph. It was during that polygraph that Montaperto made his admissions. In February 2004, FBI agents searched his home and found six 1980s-era classified documents. Montaperto pleaded guilty on 22 June 2006 to one count of unlawful retention of classified national defense information and—as a condition of the plea bargain—admitted to having provided Chinese military attachés considerable amounts of Secret and Top Secret information. Montaperto claimed that passing classified intelligence to China was unintentional and that he was only trying to gain intelligence that could be used in US policymaking. The plea bargain meant that Montaparto was not charged on more serious espionage counts. Instead he was sentenced on 8 September 2006 to three months in prison and three months' home detention, with five years' probation. Letters of support from current and former US senior intelligence and military officials persuaded the judge to grant the light sentence.

cicentre.com	6 Jul 2006, "Counterintelligence Case: Dr. Ronald N. Montaperto"
Washington Times	8 Sep 2006, "Leak Cost U.S. Spy Links to Chinese Arms Sales"
Washington Times	23 Feb 2007, "Inside the Ring"

MONTES, ANA BELEN, a senior intelligence analyst at the Defense Intelligence Agency, transmitted sensitive and classified military and intelligence information to Cuba for at least 16 years before she was arrested on 21 September 2001. Surveillance on her activities was curtailed in response to the terrorist attacks of 11 September 2001 and concern that Cuba could pass on intelligence to other nations. Montes was 44, unmarried, and a US citizen of Puerto Rican descent. She was employed by the Justice Department when sometime before 1985 she began working with the Cuban Directorate of Intelligence. It has not been revealed whether she volunteered or was recruited by them. They encouraged her to seek a position with better access to information, and in 1985 she transferred to a job at DIA. From her office at Bolling AFB in Washington, DC, she focused on Latin American military intelligence. In 1992, she shifted from her initial work on Nicaragua and became the senior DIA analyst for Cuba. She passed at least one polygraph test while engaged in espionage. Montes met her Cuban handlers every three or four months either in the US or in Cuba to exchange encrypted disks of information or instructions. The Cubans also kept in contact through encrypted high-frequency radio bursts that she received on a short wave radio. She would enter the sequences of coded numbers coming from the radio into her laptop computer, and then apply a decryption disk to them to read the messages. She used pay phones on Washington street corners to send back encrypted number sequences to pager numbers answered by Cuban officials at the United Nations. By not following their strict instructions on how to remove all traces of the messages from her computer hard disk, Montes left behind evidence of her activities. Over her years of espionage, she gave the Cubans the names of four US military intelligence agents (they escaped harm), details on at least one special access program, defense contingency planning for Cuba, and aerial surveillance photos. She had access to Intelink and the information contributed to that network by 60 agencies and departments of the Federal government. Montes cooperated in debriefings by various intelligence agencies in a plea agreement to reduce her sentence. Her lawyers claimed she spied from sympathy toward Cuba and that she received no money for her espionage other than travel expenses and the cost of her laptop. She was sentenced on 16 October 2002 to 25 years in prison and five years' probation. At the sentencing hearing she made a defiantly unrepentant statement condemning US policy towards Cuba. The judge responded that she had betrayed her family and her country and told her "If you cannot love your country, you should at least do it no harm."

Miami Herald	21 Mar 2001, "To Catch a Spy"
Miami Herald	28 Mar 2001, "Cuban Spy Passed Polygraph at Least Once"
New York Times	30 Sep 2001, "Intelligence Analyst Charged with Spying for Cuba"

Miami Herald   16 Jun 2002, "She Led Two Lives—Dutiful Analyst, and Spy for Cuba"
New York Times   17 Oct 2002, "Ex-U.S. Aide Sentenced to 25 Years for Spying for Cuba"

MOORE, EDWIN G. II, a retired CIA employee, was arrested by the FBI in 1976 and charged with espionage after attempting to sell classified documents to Soviet officials. A day earlier, an employee at a residence for Soviet personnel in Washington, DC, had discovered a package on the grounds and turned it over to police, fearing it was a bomb. The package was found to contain classified CIA documents and a note requesting that $3,000 be dropped at a specified location. The note offered more documents in exchange for $197,000. Moore was arrested after picking up what he thought to be the payment at a drop site near his home. A search of his residence yielded 10 boxes of classified CIA documents. Moore retired from the CIA in 1973 and, although financial gain was a strong motivational factor leading to espionage, it is known that he was disgruntled with his former employer due to lack of promotion. Moore pleaded not guilty by reason of insanity, but was convicted and sentenced to 15 years in prison. He was granted parole in 1979.

Washington Post   13 Apr 1977, "Thought He Was on Assignment for CIA"
Washington Post   25 Apr 1977, "Trial of Ex-Agent..."
Washington Post   6 May 1977, "Moore Guilty of Trying to Sell CIA Files"

MORISON, SAMUEL LORING, a civilian analyst with the Office of Naval Intelligence, was arrested 1 October 1984 for supplying Jane's Publications with classified photography showing a Soviet nuclear powered carrier under construction. The photographs were subsequently published in *Jane's Defence Weekly* (July 1984). Morison, described as a heavy spender and unhappy with his Navy Department job, had been employed by Jane's as a part-time contributor. A search of his apartment turned up two portions of Navy documents marked Secret. On 17 October 1985, after a seven-day trial, Morison became the first individual convicted under the 1917 Espionage Code for unauthorized disclosure to the press. Also convicted of theft of government property, Morison was sentenced to two years' imprisonment on 4 December 1985. The decision was appealed and in April 1988 the conviction was upheld by the 4th US Circuit Court of Appeals. In October 1988 the Supreme Court declined to hear the case, thus endorsing the use of the espionage code for prosecuting cases of unauthorized disclosure.

Washington Post   3 Oct 1984, "Navy Analyst Arrested in Photo Sale"
New York Times   8 Oct 1984, "Disclosing Secrets to the Press..."
Washington Post   29 Oct 1984, "Unlikely Espionage Suspect"
Washington Post   18 Oct 1985, "Morison Guilty of Spying, Stealing Documents"

MORTATI, TOMMASO, former US Army paratrooper, was arrested in Vincenza some time in 1989 by Italian authorities on charges of having passed Top Secret documents to Hungarian military intelligence services. According to European news reports, the former Army sergeant, who was born in Italy, confessed to disclosing secrets about American and NATO bases in Italy and claimed he belonged to a still-active espionage network. He is presumed to have been a member of the same network that included the Conrad spy ring in Bad Kreuznach, Germany. Conrad was arrested in August 1988 and has since been sentenced by a German court to life imprisonment. Mortati was born in Italy but later emigrated to the US where he obtained US citizenship. He left the army in 1987 but remained in Italy as his American wife continued to work for the US Army base in Vincenza. Mortati's arrest followed that of Hungarian-born naturalized American **ZOLTON SZABO** who recruited Mortati in 1981, sent him for two weeks of training in Budapest, and continued to be his contact. Mortati is said to have confessed to Italian authorities that he attempted to bribe several Italian officers in 1984 and 1985, offering money for information. Press reports state that Italy's military secret service was informed about Mortati's activities by German and Austrian counterintelligence authorities. A search of Mortati's home revealed a hidden two-way radio used to transmit his reports in code. Up until the time of his arrest, he had received $500 a month from the Hungarian Intelligence Service plus a payment for every report filed, based on its importance. Mortati was convicted in an Italian court and after a period of incarceration was released.

This summary is based on European media items and an ABC Television News report.

MURPHY, MICHAEL RICHARD, a Navy Seaman assigned to the USS *James K. Polk,* motivated by money, reportedly made several calls to the Soviet Mission to the United Nations in June 1981, offering to make a deal which he said "would benefit both the Soviets and himself." He was offered immunity from prosecution in exchange for cooperation. A polygraph examination indicated that he had contacted the Soviets three times, but had not passed any information. In August, 1981 Murphy was discharged from the Navy.

NESBITT, FRANK ARNOLD. The former Marine and Air Force communications officer was arrested by the FBI on 14 October 1989 and charged with delivering unauthorized information to the Soviet government. Nesbitt, a Memphis resident, left behind family and bewildered colleagues in June, appending a terse note to his weed trimmer ("I'm gone. Don't look for me."), and flew to Belize in Central America. Plans to settle there did not work out, so he moved on to Guatemala City where he enrolled in Spanish classes. In August while sightseeing in Sucre, Bolivia, he happened to board a bus full of Russian ballet dancers. He attended the ballet that evening and the next day bumped into a Soviet official traveling with the group. This meeting set in motion his trip to Moscow. From Sucre he went to La Paz where a Soviet Embassy official arranged for his flight to Moscow. Nesbitt claims he stayed 11 days in Moscow in a safe house, wrote from memory 32 pages detailing US defense communications, was polygraphed, toured the city, and met important KGB personnel. However, he grew upset over the Soviets' failure to grant him citizenship and provide him with an apartment and job. He returned, in a circuitous route, to Guatemala where he contacted US authorities who then accompanied him to Washington, DC. He was met by the FBI and arrested 11 days later. He offered his services as a double agent to the FBI claiming he did not give the Soviets any useful information. The National Security Agency, however, determined that information Nesbitt said he provided is still classified. The former communications officer served in the military between 1963 and 1966, and 1969 to 1979. On 8 November, he was indicted on a charge of conspiring with a Soviet agent to pass sensitive national defense information to the Soviet Union. Nesbitt initially pleaded innocent to espionage and conspiracy charges. If convicted, he faced a possible life sentence and fines up to $500,000. According to his lawyer, Nesbitt "wanted to have some excitement in his life," but it is likely that he was also motivated by money and also a sense of disgruntlement. A Soviet foreign ministry spokesman has said that Nesbitt was denied Soviet citizenship because a check of the autobiography he gave the Soviet parliament "led to suspicion of his possible connections with the criminal underworld." On 1 February 1990 Nesbitt changed his plea to guilty in order to receive a substantially reduced sentence. On 27 April he was sentenced in US District Court to 10 years in a psychiatric treatment facility at a Federal prison. His psychiatric evaluation states that he suffers from severe personality disorders.

Washington Post	15 Oct 1989, "Odyssey of a Suspected Spy; FBI Arrests Man in Va. After Moscow Trip"
Washington Post	17 Oct 1989, "No Bail for Alleged Spy"
Washington Post	20 Oct 1989, "Suspected Spy Sought to Defect, FBI Says"
Washington Post	2 Feb 1990, "Guilty Plea Entered in Secrets Case"
Washington Post	27 Apr 1990, "Ex-Officer Given 10 Years in Mental Hospital for Spying"

NICHOLSON, HAROLD JAMES, was arrested on 16 November 1996 at Dulles International Airport as he was about to board a flight to Switzerland. On his person were found rolls of film bearing images of Top Secret documents. Nicholson is the highest ranking Central Intelligence Agency officer (GS-15) charged with espionage to date. Counterintelligence officials believe that he began spying for Russian intelligence in June 1994 as he was completing a tour of duty as deputy station chief in Malaysia. He joined the agency in 1980 after serving as a captain in the US Army. Nicholson was charged with passing a wide range of highly classified information to Moscow, including biographic information on every CIA case officer trained between 1994 and 1996. He is also suspected of having compromised the identities of US and foreign business people who have provided information to the CIA. According to investigators, for two and a half years he had been hacking into the agency's computer system and providing the Russians with every secret he could steal. It is alleged that Nicholson received approximately $120,000 from the Russians over a two-year period. He came under suspicion in late 1995 when he failed a series of polygraph examinations. Further investigation revealed a pattern of extravagant spending, and an unusual pattern of foreign travel followed by large, unexplained bank deposits. Nicholson, who at the time was in the middle of a divorce and child custody battle, claimed that he did it for his children and to pay his bills. On 21 November 1996 he was indicted on one count of conspiracy to commit espionage. On 3 March 1997, Nicholson pleaded guilty under a plea agreement in which he admitted that he had been a Russian spy. On 6 June he was sentenced by a Federal judge to 23 years and seven months in prison. This reduced sentence reflected his extensive cooperation with government investigators.

Los Angeles Times	19 Nov 1996, "Career CIA Officer Is Charged With Spying For Russia"
Los Angeles Times	21 Nov 1996, "Alleged Mole To Plead Not Guilty"
New York Times	4 Mar 1997, "C.I.A. Officer Admits Spying For Russians"
Washington Post	6 Jun 1997, "Convicted Spy Says He Did It For His Family"

NOUR, ALMALIKI, in 1998 used a false identity on forms applying for US citizenship. In 2003 he used the same alias to get a position as an Arabic translator for the L-3 Titan Corporation, which provides translation services in Iraq for US military personnel. Once working for Titan, he was granted Secret and Top Secret security clearances based on the same false identity. Later, in 2004 during his second year-long assignment as a translator and interpreter in an intelligence unit of the 82nd Airborne Division in Iraq in the Sunni Triangle, Nour took several classified documents from the US Army without authorization. These included the coordinates of insurgents' locations which the US Army was targeting and plans for protecting Sunnis on their pilgrimage to Mecca. He also photographed a classified battle map of a base near Najaf. In September 2005, and apparently in response to some security concern, the FBI and military investigators first interviewed Nour in Iraq. He was arrested the same month at his apartment in Brooklyn, New York, and was charged the next month with lying to federal officials on three occasions: on his naturalization application (he became naturalized February 2000), on his application for a security clearance (2003), and in interviews connected with the renewal of his clearance. It is unclear what specifically brought Nour to the investigators' attention, but he had originally claimed to have been a Lebanese born in 1960, that he had never married, and that his parents had been killed in Beirut, all untrue. After his arrest, Nour admitted that he was actually Moroccan, born in 1959 and married, and that his parents were alive and living in Morocco. A search of his apartment by the FBI's Joint Terrorism Task Force turned up a Moroccan power of attorney and other records showing that he had wired large sums of money (equal to a year's salary) to a woman in Morocco believed to be his wife. It was during this search that investigators found the classified documents taken from Iraq. An official for the New York FBI said: "He lied to attain his U.S. citizenship. He lied to gain employment with a government contractor. And he lied to obtain security clearances. Through serial deception an eminently untrustworthy person inveigled his way into a position of trust, and he abused that trust." Nour was not charged with terrorism or espionage. He had first pleaded guilty in December 2005 to using a false identity to acquire US citizenship. Later, on 14 February 2007, he pleaded guilty to being in unauthorized possession of classified documents. On 19 May 2008, he was sentenced to 10 years and one month in prison and was stripped of his citizenship.

Washington Times	22 Oct 2005, "Linguist in Iraq Accused of Fraud"
Washington Post	15 Feb 2007, "Translator Who Faked Identity Pleads Guilty to Having Secret Data"
Department of Justice	19 May 2008, "U.S. Army Translator Sentenced to 121 Months' Imprisonment..."

OAKLEY, ROY LYNN, 67, was formerly employed as a laborer and security escort by Bechtel Jacobs at the East Tennessee Technology Park (ETTP) in Oakridge, Tennessee. The plant had previously been operated by the Department of Energy as a facility to produce highly enriched uranium. The plant was closed in 1987 and turned over Bechtel Jacobs for cleanup. While employed at ETTP in 2006 and 2007, Oakley had a security clearance that permitted him access to classified and protected materials, including instruments, appliances and information related to the gaseous diffusion process for enriching uranium. Some of these items were classified as Restricted. For reasons unclear in open sources, the FBI initiated an undercover investigation against Oakley and, in January 2007, contacted him using an undercover agent assuming the role of an agent of a foreign government. In telephone calls and face-to-face meetings with the undercover agent, Oakley had stated that he had taken certain parts of uranium enrichment fuel rods or tubes and other associated hardware items from the ETTP and that he wanted to sell these materials for $200,000 to the foreign government. Once he had handed over the materials to the agent and had been given $200,000, Oakley was confronted by FBI agents and admitted to trying to sell these materials. He had no contact with actual foreign governments, terrorists or criminal groups and appeared to have been motivated solely by greed. Oakley was indicted in July 2007. On 26 January 2009, the day his trial was slated to begin, Oakley pleaded guilty to Count 1 of the indictment charging him with unlawful disclosure of Restricted Data under the Atomic Energy Act. On 18 June 2009, Oakley was sentenced to six years in prison, after which he will be on supervised release for three years.

New York Times	20 Jul 2007, "Worker Indicted on Charges of Trying to Sell Nuclear Equipment"
Department of Justice, News Release	26 Jan 2009, "Former Oak Ridge Complex Employee Pleads Guilty to Unlawful Disclosure of Restricted Atomic Energy Data"

OTT, BRUCE DAMIAN, Airman 1st Class, assigned duties as an administrative clerk at Beale Air Force Base, was arrested 22 January 1986 by FBI and Air Force security agents at a Davis, California, motel as he attempted to sell classified information to undercover agents posing as Soviet representatives. One of the documents cited is "The SAC Tactical Doctrine for SR-71 Crews." At that time, Beale AFB was the home base of SR-71 "Blackbird" reconnaissance aircraft. It is reported that Ott tried to contact representatives at the Soviet Consulate in San Francisco during the month of January. His communication was intercepted and no classified information actually changed hands. Military prosecutors contended that Ott hoped to be paid up to $160,000 for his information. Following an eight-day court-martial proceeding, Ott was found guilty and on 7 August was sentenced to 25 years in prison.

New York Times	29 Jan 1986, "Airman in California Charged in New Spy Case"
New York Times	1 Feb 1986, "Details are given on Spying Charge"

PAKHTUSOV, YURI N., a lieutenant colonel in the Soviet army, arrived in the US in June 1988, as assistant military attaché with the Soviet Military Mission. Two months later he began approaching an American employee of a defense contractor to obtain documents dealing with how the US government protects classified and other sensitive information contained in its computer systems. What he did not know was that the American reported the approaches to US authorities. Pakhtusov, 35, was caught as part of a sting operation after he received classified documents from the American employee working under FBI control. On 9 March 1989, he was ordered out of the country and declared *persona non grata.*

St. Louis Post-Dispatch   11 Mar 1989, "Soviet Diplomat Ousted As Spy"

PELTON, RONALD WILLIAM, communications specialist with the National Security Agency for 14 years, was identified as a spy for the Soviet Union based on facts provided by a defector. He was arrested in Annapolis, MD, on 25 November 1985. During his employment at NSA, Pelton had access to information on a wide range of highly classified projects. He was said to be a highly skilled technician and fluent in the Russian language but a poor manager of his personal finances. Three months before resigning from his agency, Pelton declared personal bankruptcy, listing debts of over $65,000. While at NSA he expressed hostility toward the agency and dissatisfaction with his position. Failing at several subsequent jobs and with only a few hundred dollars in the bank, Pelton walked into the Soviet Embassy in January 1980 and offered his services to the KGB for money. He was debriefed at length and provided highly classified information about US intelligence collection locations. He also made several trips to Vienna, Austria, to speak with Soviet agents. According to reports in the media, no documents were passed by Pelton; however, former coworkers stated that he had an excellent memory and an encyclopedic knowledge of intelligence activities carried out by the agency. He allegedly received $35,000 from the Soviets between 1980 and 1983 for information about classified US intelligence collection programs targeting the Soviet Union. In July 1985, the KGB colonel who had initial contact with Pelton in Washington, DC, Vitaly Yurchenko, defected to the US and provided information that led to his prosecution. At the time of his arrest, Pelton admitted selling intelligence information to the Soviet Union. He was indicted 20 December 1985 on six counts related to espionage. Despite his statement at the time of arrest, Pelton pleaded not guilty. Following a highly publicized trial, he was convicted on 5 June 1986 on one count of conspiracy and two counts of espionage. On 6 December 1986 Pelton was sentenced to three concurrent life sentences.

Washington Post   26 Nov 1985, "FBI Says Spy Suspect Admits Selling Data*"*
New York Times   28 Nov 1985, "Ex-Security Agency Employee Said to Have Admitted Spying"
Washington Post   7 Dec 1985, "Accused Spy Ronald Pelton Was Preoccupied with Money"
Washington Post   6 Jun 1986, "Pelton Spy Case Chronology"

PERI, MICHAEL A., 22, an electronic warfare signals specialist for the Army, fled to East Germany with a laptop computer and military secrets 20 February 1989and voluntarily returned 4 March 1989 to plead guilty to espionage. He was sentenced to 30 years in a military prison. Even after his court-martial, authorities were at a loss to explain what happened. Peri said he made an impulsive mistake, that he felt overworked and unappreciated in his job for the 11th Armored Cavalry Regiment in Fulda, West Germany. His work involved operating equipment that detects enemy radar and other signals. Peri had been described as "a good, clean-cut soldier" with a "perfect record." During his tour of duty in Germany he had been promoted and twice was nominated for a soldier of the month award.

St. Louis Post-Dispatch   25 Jun 1989, "US Soldier Given 30 Years"
Los Angeles Times   29 Jun 1989, "From Soldier to Spy; A Baffling About-Face"

PICKERING, JEFFERY LORING. On 7 June 1983, an individual using the name Christopher Eric Loring entered the Naval Regional Medical Center, Seattle, Washington, acting very erratic and stating that he possessed a large quantity of "secret documents vital to the security of our country." The individual was in possession of one plastic addressograph card imprinted with the address of the Soviet Embassy, Washington, DC. During permissive searches of his car and residence by Naval Investigative Service agents, four government-marked envelopes containing classified microfiche and 147 microfiche cards containing a variety of classified defense publications were located. Through investigation, the individual was identified as Jeffery Loring Pickering, who had previously served in the US Marine Corps. During his Marine enlistment, he was described as a thief, thrill seeker, and a perpetual liar. Pickering left the Marines in August 1973, but became dissatisfied with civilian life and began efforts to re-enlist in the military. Pickering assumed an alias, Christopher Eric Loring, hid the facts of his prior Marine Corps affiliation, and enlisted in the US Navy on 23 January 1979. During interrogation, Pickering admitted stealing the classified material from the ship's office of the USS *Fanning* between July and October 1982. Pickering likewise expressed an interest in the KGB, and said he fantasized about espionage. He ultimately admitted mailing a five-page Secret document to the Soviet Embassy, Washington, DC, along with a typed letter offering additional classified material to the Soviet Union. On 3 October 1983, Pickering pleaded guilty at a general court-martial to several violations including espionage. Pickering was convicted and sentenced to five years at hard labor, forfeiture of $400 per month for 60 months, reduction to E-1, and a bad conduct discharge.

Naval Investigative Service Command, *Espionage*, 1989

PITTS, EARL EDWIN, a senior FBI agent, was arrested on 18 December 1996 at the FBI Academy in Quantico, Virginia, and charged with providing classified information to the Russian intelligence services from 1987 until 1992. He is believed to have received $224,000 from Russian intelligence services for his activities. Pitts allegedly turned over Top Secret documents to the KGB (and after the collapse of the Soviet Union, the SVRR), including a list of FBI assets who were providing intelligence on Russia. Pitts' betrayal of trust began in July 1987 when, as a newly assigned agent to the New York City field office, he wrote to a Soviet representative assigned to the Soviet Mission at the United Nations and asked to meet a KGB officer. From 1988 to 1992 Pitts allegedly, on nine occasions, provided documents to his handler, KGB officer Aleksandr Karpov. Each meeting was followed by an unexplained deposit in one of several bank accounts in the Washington area. After 1992 Pitts became inactive as a foreign agent. He was identified as a mole when Karpov himself became a double agent for the FBI. At this time the FBI set up a sting operation against Pitts and, using agents posing as Russians, easily gained his agreement to renew his espionage activities. Over a period of 15 months, Pitts made 22 drops of classified documents to undercover FBI agents and was paid $65,000. The FBI was also informed of Pitts' involvement by his wife, Mary Colombaro Pitts, who confided her suspicions about her husband's activities to another FBI agent. Earl Edwin Pitts pleaded guilty to two counts of espionage in February 1997 following the discovery of a computer disk with a letter to his supposed Russian handler. On 23 June, he was sentenced to 27 years in prison by a Federal judge who stated that the former agent was guilty of "the most egregious abuse of trust." When asked why he spied, Pitts cited a number of grievances he had against the FBI and stated that he "wanted to pay them back."

Washington Post	19 Dec 1996, "Senior FBI Agent Charged With Spying for Russians"
Washington Post	19 Dec 1996, "Espionage Suspect Depicted as Eager to Sell His Loyalty"
Washington Post	2 Mar 1997, "Spy Case Sealed by 1990 Letter; Computer Disk Held Agent's Memo to KGB"
Washington Post	24 Jun 1997, "Ex-FBI Agent Gets 27 Years for Passing Secrets to Moscow"

POLLARD, JONATHAN JAY, a civilian counterintelligence analyst at the Anti-Terrorist Alert Center at the Naval Investigative Service in Suitland, MD, and his wife, **ANNE HENDERSON-POLLARD**, were apprehended on 21 November 1985 outside the Israeli Embassy in Washington, DC, as they vainly sought political asylum with hope of fleeing the country. Both were charged under the espionage code for selling classified documents to an Israeli intelligence unit for $50,000. It is reported that Pollard's detection resulted from tips from fellow employees that the accused was seeking and copying more classified documents than his job required. His pattern of taking documents away from the office was noted by a supervisor. Confronted with evidence of his activities by the NCIS and the FBI on 15 November, Pollard admitted delivering classified documents to a foreign government agent. He was originally ideologically motivated to pass classified information, but that motivation was later clouded by monetary considerations. The couple had begun to lead a luxurious lifestyle based on their monthly retainer from Israel of $2,500. They visited Israel and Europe several times at the expense of the Israeli government and on one of these trips were married in Vienna, Austria. While at Stanford University in 1976, Pollard is reported to have boasted to friends about working for the Mossad, Israel's foreign intelligence agency. Pollard's claim to involvement with Israeli intelligence never emerged during the course a background investigation when he applied for a Top Secret security clearance. Anne Henderson-Pollard was accused of intending to sell to representatives of the Peoples Republic of China documents related to the US analysis of China's intelligence operations in this country. A suitcase found in their residence was filled with Top Secret documents relating to military capabilities of foreign countries. On 4 June 1986, Pollard and his wife pleaded guilty to espionage and related charges under a plea agreement with Federal officials. Four Israeli nationals were later named as unindicted co-conspirators. On 4 March 1987 Jonathan Pollard was sentenced to life imprisonment. Several attempts by special interest groups to obtain a parole for Pollard have failed. Anne Henderson-Pollard received a five-year term.

New York Times   28 Nov 1985, "F.B.I. Man Says Naval Analyst Told of Spying"
Washington Post   4 Dec 1985, "FBI Seeking Pollard Contact Identity"
Washington Post   5 Jun 1986, "Ex-Analyst Pollard Pleads Guilty to Spying"
Naval Investigative Service Command, *Espionage*, 1989

RAMSAY, RODERICK JAMES, a former US Army sergeant, was arrested in Tampa, Florida, on 7 June 1990 and charged with conspiracy to commit espionage. Ramsay joined the Army in 1981 and was transferred to West Germany in June 1983 where he was recruited by then-Army Sgt. **CLYDE LEE CONRAD**. (Conrad was sentenced to life imprisonment in May 1990 for treason.) Ramsay received $20,000 for selling military secrets that could have caused the collapse of NATO—Top Secret plans for the defense of Central Europe, location and use of NATO tactical nuclear weapons, and the ability of NATO's military communications—that were passed to Hungary and Czechoslovakia. An FBI official said, "It's one of the most serious breaches ever—it's unprecedented what went over to the other side. The ability to defend ourselves is neutralized because they have all our plans." Ramsay initially used a 35-millimeter camera to photograph classified documents, but then switched to more effective videotape. He reportedly recorded a total of about 45 hours of videotape. Ramsay is said to have a high IQ, is multilingual, and has the "ability to recall minute details, facts and figures from hundreds of volumes of documents." The FBI described him as "brilliant but erratic." In West Germany he worked as a clerk-typist in the 8th Infantry Division. When arrested he was unemployed, living sometimes at his mother's house and sometimes in his car. In September 1991 he pleaded guilty and agreed to cooperate with prosecutors. On 28 August 1992 he was sentenced to 36 years in prison. The sentence reflects his cooperation with investigators. According to the FBI, this case was the most extensive espionage investigation in the history of the FBI and considered to be the largest US espionage conspiracy case in modern history.

Los Angeles Times   9 Jun 1990, "Alleged Spy Called Brilliant, Erratic"
Washington Times   29 Aug 1992, "Spying Sergeant Gets 36 Years"
DoD Security Institute, *Security Awareness Bulletin*, No. 1-97, January 1997, "Profile of a Spy"

RATKAI, STEPHEN JOSEPH, was arrested by Canadian authorities on 11 June 1988 and charged with attempting to obtain US classified military documents related to the operation of a US Navy installation at Argentia, Newfoundland. Although born in Canada, Ratkai was brought up in Hungary, his father's native country, after the death of his Canadian mother. As an adult he returned to Canada to work as a short-order cook, but made frequent trips back to Hungary. Ratkai was seized as a result of a double agent operation begun two years earlier by the US Naval Investigative Service and Canadian intelligence: On 2 December 1986 Donna Geiger walked on board a Soviet scientific research vessel, the *Akademik Boris Petrov*, which was temporarily docked in the harbor of St. John's, Newfoundland. Geiger, a Navy lieutenant, was a double agent who had been recruited by the Naval Investigative Service. She was stationed at the US Naval Facility in Argentia. On board the Soviet ship, she portrayed herself as a "disgruntled female naval officer ... working in a world dominated by men ... assigned to an isolated duty station." She brought classified material to prove her intentions. Two months later she received a letter indicating someone would meet with her. Finally in May 1987, acting on directions she received by mail, she met her contact, "Michael," in the parking lot of the Hotel Newfoundland in St. John's. She was given money and some tasking to collect information. A week later Lt. Geiger met Michael in a restaurant. Classified information was exchanged for money. During this meeting she was tasked to provide information on the highly classified Sound Underwater Surveillance System, the Naval Facility Argentia's area of responsibility. After several more meetings, Michael was identified as Ratkai. At their last meeting in June 1988, Geiger steered Ratkai to a room at the Hotel Newfoundland which was outfitted with surveillance equipment. More money and classified information was exchanged. When Ratkai left the room, he was arrested. No damage is reported to have occurred. On 6 February 1989 Ratkai pleaded guilty to one general charge of spying on behalf of the Soviet Union from May 1987 to June 1988 and one charge of attempted espionage. On 9 March 1989 the Newfoundland Supreme Court sentenced Ratkai to two concurrent nine-year prison terms.

New York Times   16 Jun 1988, "Canada Holds Suspect in Spying on US Navy"
St. Louis Post-Dispatch   11 Mar 1989, "Spy Gets 9 Years"
Naval Investigative Service Command, *Espionage*, 1989

REGAN, BRIAN PATRICK, a former Air Force intelligence analyst, was arrested on 3 August 2001, at Dulles International Airport as he was boarding a flight for Switzerland. On his person he was carrying missile site information on Iraq and contact information for embassies in Switzerland. Regan, who had enlisted in the Air Force at 17, began working for the National Reconnaissance Office in 1995 where he administered the Intelink, a classified web network for the intelligence community. Following his retirement from the military as a Master Sergeant in 2001, he was employed by defense contractor TRW and resumed work at NRO where he was employed at the time of his arrest. Regan had held a Top Secret clearance since 1980. Computers searched in Regan's home led to the discovery of letters offering to sell secrets to Libya, Iraq, and China. In the Iraq case, he asked Saddam Hussein for $13 million. At his arraignment on November 5, 2001, he pleaded not guilty to three counts of attempting to market highly classified documents and one count of gathering national defense information. The documents, classified at the Top Secret SCI level, concerned the US satellite program, early warning systems, and communications intelligence information. Regan is thought to have been motivated not only by money (he had very heavy personal debts), but also by a sense of disgruntlement, complaining frequently to former coworkers and neighbors about his job and station in life. On 20 February 2003, Regan was convicted of all charges except attempting to sell secrets to Libya, and on 21 March, under a sentencing agreement, he was sentenced to life imprisonment without parole. Information provided by Regan after sentencing led FBI and NRO investigators to 19 sites in rural Virginia and Maryland where he had buried over 20,000 pages of classified documents, five CDs, and five videotapes that he had stashed presumably for future sales.

Washington Post   24 Aug 2001, "Retired Air Force Sgt. Charged with Espionage"
Washington Post   21 Feb 2003, "Analyst Convicted in Spy Case; Regan Jury
              Yet to Decide if Death Penalty Applies"
New York Times   21 Mar 2003, "Life Sentence for Bid to Sell Secrets to Iraq"
Los Angeles Times   31 Jul 2003, "Arduous Dig to Find Spy's Buried Stash;
              Agents Search Virginia, Maryland Park Sites under Rough Conditions,
              Recover All Documents"

RICHARDSON, DANIEL WALTER, a US Army sergeant stationed at the Aberdeen Proving Ground, Maryland, was arrested on 7 January 1988 and charged with attempting to spy for the Soviet Union. Richardson reportedly intended to offer unspecified national defense information to Soviet representatives in exchange for money. No information is believed to have been compromised. Officials stated that Richardson was apprehended after electronic surveillance picked up his efforts to contact Soviet representatives. This led to his negotiation with an undercover government agent posing as a Soviet. He was arrested at the Holiday Inn in Aberdeen (with an unclassified military manual and circuitry from the M-1 tank in his possession) as he attempted to meet with the undercover agent. An Army spokesman stated that Richardson had a Secret clearance but "no ready access to classified materials." Although trained as an instructor, his job was to issue tools to students at the Ordinance Center School at Aberdeen. "Money and revenge against the military" have been identified by an administration official as Richardson's chief motivations for espionage. Described as a mediocre soldier, Richardson was demoted in August 1987 for repeated tardiness. He was charged at the time of arrest with espionage, failure to report contacts with a foreign government, theft, and unauthorized disposition of government property. On 26 August 1988 Richardson was sentenced by a military jury to 10 years in prison, fined $36,000, and discharged with a bad conduct record.

New York Times   15 Jan 1988, "Army Sergeant is Arrested on Espionage Charges"
Washington Post   16 Jan 1988, "Soldier Had No Access to Army Secrets"

ROGALSKY, IVAN N., a former Soviet merchant seaman admitted to the US as a political refugee, was arrested in New Jersey on 7 January 1977 after receiving a classified document from a cleared employee of RCA Research Center. The employee, who worked on communications satellite and defense projects, agreed to work under FBI control after first being approached by Rogalsky. The ex-seaman had earlier asked the RCA employee for unclassified information about the space shuttle program. A second secretary of the Soviet Mission to the United Nations, **YEVEGENY P. KARPOV**, was named as a co-conspirator. Karpov had been suspected of being a KGB officer by the FBI. According to later press reports, Rogalsky was not tried due to questions regarding his sanity. He claimed to receive instructions from disembodied voices.

New York Times   8 Jan 1977, "Soviet Alien Arrested in Jersey on Spy Charges"
New York Times   9 Jan 1977, "Accused Soviet Spy Known as a Drifter"
New York Times   16 Jan 1977, "Spy Case Clouds a Russian Holiday"

RONDEAU, JEFFREY STEPHEN, a US Army sergeant stationed at Bangor, Maine, was arrested in Tampa, Florida, on 22 October 1992, and charged with espionage for providing Army and NATO defense secrets, including tactical nuclear weapons plans, to intelligence agents of Hungary and Czechoslovakia from 1985 through 1988. Rondeau was allegedly part of the Conrad spy ring which operated out of the

8th Infantry Division, Bad Kreuznach, Germany, in the mid-1980s. A German court convicted former US Army sergeant **CLYDE LEE CONRAD** of high treason in 1990 and sentenced him to life in prison. The inquiry into Rondeau's involvement was aided by the cooperation of **RODERICK JAMES RAMSAY**. In 1991, Ramsey, also a former Army sergeant stationed in Germany, was sentenced to 36 years in prison by an American court for his involvement in the ring. As a recognition signal, Ramsay reportedly gave Rondeau a torn dollar bill to use when dealing with others in the plot. The US Attorney for the Middle District of Florida said, "The espionage charge in this case is especially serious because it related to the allied defense of Central Europe including the use of tactical nuclear weapons and military communications." The three-count indictment of Rondeau charged that he conspired with Conrad, Ramsay, and others to "copy, steal, photograph, and videotape" documents and sell them to Hungary and Czechoslovakia. The indictment did not specify what amount of money he may have received. On 28 March 1994, Rondeau pleaded guilty to espionage. In June, 1994, Rondeau, along with Sgt. **JEFFERY EUGENE GREGORY**, another member of the espionage ring, was sentenced by a military court to 18 years in prison.

Houston Chronicle   23 Oct 1992, "US Soldier is Charged with Spying"
Atlanta Constitution   23 Oct 1992, "Soldier Accused of Selling NATO Plans to Communists"

ROTH, JOHN REECE, 70, a retired University of Tennessee (UT) professor and expert on plasma physics, was indicted in May 2008 for illegally exporting to China sensitive, restricted, military information related to plasma technology designed to be deployed on the wings of drones. Dr. Roth was accused of passing information to the Chinese research assistant working on the contract, a doctoral candidate at UT. Roth was also accused of taking reports and related studies in his laptop to China during a lecture tour in 2006 and having one restricted report emailed to him there through a Chinese professor's Internet connection. The indictment alleged, among other things, that Roth did not obtain permission to take the sensitive documents to China and lied to the Defense Department about his employment of a Chinese graduate student (he also employed graduate students from Iran and UK). All this activity was in violation of the Arms Export Control Act (AECA). In 2004, Roth became a subcontractor to Atmospheric Glow Technology, Inc. (AGT), a spin-off of UT to market commercial applications of UT's plasma sciences lab that Roth had previously headed. The company had been granted a US Air Force contract. Because of the sensitive nature of the program, the parties allegedly agreed that no foreign nationals would work on the project. And in fact Roth first hired an American student to handle the export control data and the Chinese student to work on nonsensitive materials in the lab. That plan fell apart, however, when the arrangement slowed down progress, and soon the two students began sharing information. Roth was told by university officials that he was violating the law in allowing foreign nationals to work on a military defense project. Roth, on the other hand, believed that a project only became export-controlled when the research had netted an actual product; and in this case, the work was not finished. A federal jury convicted Roth on 3 September 2008 on 18 counts of conspiracy, fraud, and violating the AECA. The former director of plasma science at AGT, **DANIEL SHERMAN**, and AGT itself, were also indicted and both have entered into plea bargains. Sherman pleaded guilty in June 2009 and will be sentenced 28 July 2009. UT cooperated in the investigation and was listed as a victim in one of the charges against Roth. This is one of the first cases in which the government has sought to punish an individual or organization for distributing scientific know-how (rather than equipment) to foreign graduate students working on military research contracts in violation of the AECA. Roth was sentenced on 1 July 2009 to 4 years in prison for passing sensitive defense information to two foreign national research assistants, one from Iran and another from China.

cicentre.com   n.d., "Roth, J. Reece"
Knoxville News Sentinel   26 Aug 2008, "Roth was Warned, Lawyers Allege"
Knoxville News Sentinel   3 Sep 2008, "Roth's Mind-Set on Trial"

Philosophy of Science Portal (philosophyofscenceportal. blogspot.com)	4 Sep 2008, "J. Reece Roth Conviction"
Washington Post	4 Sep 2008, "Professor is Convicted of Sharing Technology"
WorldTribune.com	16 Sep 2008, "China Got Strategic Drone Tech From Grad Student in Tennessee Spy Case"

SANTOS, JOSEPH, 38, an American citizen, and his Cuban wife **AMARYLIS SILVERIO SANTOS**, 37, were members of the Red Wasp Network, a spy ring operating for Cuba in south Florida from 1992 through 1998. [See also Alejandro Alonso, Linda Hernandez, and Gerardo Hernandez.] The couple was assigned by the Cuban Intelligence Service to get jobs with the US Southern Command in Miami in order to collect and pass along information and observations. They did not manage to get these jobs, although they submitted at least one report to Cuban intelligence based on observations from outside the military base. At the time of their arrest on 12 September 1998, Joseph worked as a maintenance man for a Miami sports stadium and Amarylis kept house and took care of their six-year-old daughter. On 4 February 2000 in US District court in Miami, they pled guilty in a plea bargain to being unregistered agents of a foreign government. Joseph was sentenced to four years and Amarylis to three and a half years in prison.

Independent (UK)	16 Sep 1998, "Cuban Infiltrated US Military Base, Says FBI"
Miami Herald	3 Feb 2000, "Contrite Cuban Spy Couple Sentenced"
Fort Lauderdale Sun-Sentinel	4 Feb 2000, "Couple Guilty of Espionage Get Jail Sentence"

SCHOOF, CHARLES EDWARD, 20, and **JOHN JOSEPH HAEGER**, 19, both Navy Petty Officers 3rd Class, were arrested aboard ship on 1 December 1989 on charges they conspired to commit espionage. The two sailors were stationed aboard the tank landing ship USS *Fairfax County* assigned to the Norfolk area. Both were operations specialists, trained in radar communications, electronic countermeasures, and navigational plotting. Although Schoof was reported to be the instigator of this scheme to make money, it was Haeger who had the combination to the document safe. Schoof called the Soviet Embassy in Washington, DC, to ask if someone would come down to pick up the classified material, but Norfolk is beyond the embassy's allowed travel radius. He then visited several bars looking for a ride to the embassy. A shipmate reported Schoof's activities to the ship's commanding officer. It is believed that no information was passed to the Soviets and that all documents were retrieved. On 24 April 1990, Schoof was sentenced to 25 years' imprisonment, stripped of all rank, forfeited all pay and allowances, and received a dishonorable discharge. Haeger was sentenced to 19 years, also forfeited pay and allowances and received a dishonorable discharge. Under a 1987 regulation that revised parole guidelines, the two were expected to serve virtually all of their sentences.

| Northern Virginia Sun | 11 Dec 1989, "Two Radar Operators from Landing Ship Charged in Spying Conspiracy" |
| Free Lance-Star | 26 Apr 1990, "Navy Men Get Prison Terms for Attempted Espionage" |

SCHWARTZ, MICHAEL STEPHEN, US Navy Lieutenant Commander, was charged with passing Department of Defense classified documents and computer diskettes to Saudi naval officers between November 1992 and September 1994 while assigned to a US military training mission in Riyadh, Saudi Arabia. Schwartz, a naval surface warfare officer who served in the Gulf War, was charged with four counts of espionage on 23 May 1995. He is also charged with five counts of violating Federal regulations for allegedly removing classified material to his residence. The charges resulted from a Naval Criminal Investigative Service investigation which began in September 1994. The documents allegedly included classified messages to foreign countries, military intelligence digests, intelligence advisories, and tactical intelligence summaries classified up to the Secret (Noforn) level. There is no indication that Schwartz received any money for the materials; according to a media report, Schwartz was attempting to be helpful to the Saudis because of US-Saudi cooperation during the Gulf War. On 14 October, Schwartz agreed to a plea bargain that allowed him to avoid a court-martial and possible imprisonment. According to the agreement, in November 1995, Schwartz received an "other than honorable" discharge and lost all retirement benefits and other military privileges.

Virginian-Pilot (Norfolk VA)	25 May 1995, "Officer Spied for Saudis, Navy Says"
Washington Jewish Week	1 Jun 1995, "Navy Officer Arrested on Charges of Espionage"
Washington Post	13 Sep 1995, "Norfolk Naval Officer Faces Court-Martial in Espionage Case"
Virginian-Pilot	14 Oct 1995, "Navy Officer Accused of Spying Gives U Retirement Benefits"

SCRANAGE, SHARON MARIE, operations support assistant for the CIA stationed in Ghana and her Ghanaian boyfriend, **MICHAEL SOUSSOUDIS**, were charged on 11 July 1985 with turning over classified information, including the identities of CIA agents and informants, to Ghanaian intelligence officials. It is reported that a routine polygraph test given to Scranage on her return to the US aroused CIA suspicions. Following an internal investigation, Scranage agreed to cooperate with the FBI in order to arrest Soussoudis, a business consultant and permanent resident of the US. According to one report, damaging information on CIA intelligence collection activities is likely to have been passed on by pro-Marxist Kojo Tsikata, head of Ghanaian intelligence, to Cuba, Libya, East Germany and other Soviet Bloc nations. Scranage was likely encouraged to pass along these documents by Soussoudis with whom she was intimately friendly. Indicted on 18 counts of providing classified information to a foreign country, Scranage subsequently pleaded guilty to one count under the espionage code and two counts of violating the Intelligence Identities Protection Act. Fifteen remaining charges were dropped. On 26 November Scranage was sentenced to five years in prison. (This was later reduced to two years.) At the same time Soussoudis, who had been charged with eight counts of espionage, pleaded *nolo contendere* and was sentenced to 20 years. His sentence was suspended on the condition that he leave the US within 24 hours.

Washington Post	12 Jul 1985, "CIA Aide, Ghanaian Face Spy Counts"
Washington Post	14 Jul 1985, "Routine Polygraph Opened Ghanaian Espionage Probe"
Washington Post	20 Jul 1985, "FBI Says Spying Occurred After CIA Order on Ghanaian"

SELDON, PHILLIP TYLER, a former Pentagon civilian employee, pleaded guilty on 7 August 1996 in Alexandria, Virginia, to passing classified documents to a Salvadoran air force officer while on active military duty in El Salvador as a US Army captain. After leaving the Army, Seldon took a civilian job with the Department of Defense. According to court documents, Seldon gave the Salvadoran three packets of documents between November 1992 and July 1993. None of the material was reported to have exceeded the Secret level. Seldon claimed that he had met the Salvadoran officer while working as an intelligence advisor, and he believed that the officer had the appropriate clearance. This information came to light in the course of a polygraph examination as Seldon was applying for a position with the CIA. On 8 November, Seldon was sentenced by a US District court to two years in prison.

Washington Post	9 Nov 1996, "Ex-Pentagon Worker Given 2 Years for Passing Secrets"

SHAABAN, HAFIZ AHMAD ALI SHAABAN, a 52-year-old a truck driver in Greenfield, Indiana, was arrested on 1 March 2005, accused of traveling to Iraq prior to the 2003 US invasion and offering to sell the names of US intelligence operatives in that country to agents of Saddam Hussein's Iraqi Intelligence Service. In a bugged hotel room in Baghdad he promised to acquire these names from a third party and demanded $3,000,000 as payment. (The deal fell apart after Shaaban returned to the US and could not produce the promised documents.) He also sought to gain Iraqi support to establish an Arabic TV station in the US that would broadcast pro-Iraqi material and he offered to organize volunteers to act as human shields to protect Iraqi infrastructure in the coming war. Shaaban, a Palestinian who was born in Jordan, became a naturalized US citizen by using fraudulent identification. He is believed to have been in the US since 1993. Earlier, in 1972, he had lived in Moscow where he married his first wife whose whereabouts are now unknown. The prosecution alleged that during his stay in Moscow Shaaban received training from Russian intelligence agents. One news report suggested that he had been a Soviet-trained mining engineer, another that he actually held Russian citizenship. The jury rejected Shaaban's claims that prosecutors had him confused with a dead twin brother and that the CIA had sent him to Iraq as part of a "psychological war" preceding the US invasion in 2003. Shaaban, who refused legal counsel and defended himself in court, was found guilty of conspiracy against the US, acting as a foreign agent without notification to the US Attorney General, violation of sanctions against Iraqi under the International Emergency Economic Powers Act, unlawful procurement of an identification document, fraudulently acquiring US naturalization, and tampering with a witness. Shaaban was sentenced 27 May 2006 to 13 years and four months in prison and is now incarcerated in the maximum-security prison in Colorado, far from his second wife and son who still live in Indiana. He has been stripped of his US citizenship.

| US Department of Justice | 25 Jan 2006, "Local Man Convicted of Working with Former Iraqi Intelligence Officers" |
| *Indianapolis Star* | 6 Nov 2006, "Convicted in Spy Case, Locked Away in Secrecy" |

SHU, QUAN-SHENG, 68, a Ph.D. physicist, a naturalized US citizen born in Shanghai, was president, secretary and treasurer of AMAC International, a high-tech company with offices in Beijing. The R&D company was based at the Applied Research Center in Newport News, Virginia. Shu was arrested in September 2008 and pleaded guilty 17 November 2008 to charges that he illegally exported sensitive space launch technical data and defense services to the People's Republic of China (PRC) and offered bribes to Chinese government officials. He admitted that from 2003 through October 2007 he violated the US arms export control law by providing the PRC with assistance in the design and development of a cryogenic fueling system for space launch vehicles. He also admitted that in 2003 he violated the same law by exporting to China military technical data from a document about designing and making a liquid hydrogen tank and various pumps, valves, filters and instruments. At the same time Shu pleaded guilty to offering bribes of nearly $190,000, on behalf of a French company that he represented, to Chinese government officials to win a $4 million contract for a hydrogen liquefier project. Shu was sentenced 7 April 2009 to 51 months in prison.

Digitajournal.com	25 Sep 2008, "More Chinese Espionage Involving Rocket Plans"
Department of Justice, News Release	17 Nov 2008, "Virginia Physicist Pleads Guilty To Illegally Exporting Space Launch Data to China and Offering Bribes to Chinese"
Washington Post	9 Apr 2009, "Physicist Sentenced to Prison for Helping China"

SLATTEN, CHARLES DALE, a US Army PFC in the 8th Signal Battalion of the 8th Infantry Division, was stationed at Bad Kreuznach, West Germany, in 1984. On April 14 he was arrested by the USACIDC for stealing a cryptological device with intent to sell it to the USSR. Slatten worked as a telephone installer at the Rose Barracks where he had access to the device. Although he collaborated with two friends in a scheme to sell the equipment to the Russians for an offer of $1.8 million, Slatten was the only one convicted of espionage by a military court-martial on August 22, 1984. He was sentenced to nine years in prison and given a dishonorable discharge. His motive for committing espionage at the age of 19, two years into his Army career, was money. After serving eight years of his sentence for espionage in a military prison in Kansas, Slatten was released and eventually moved to St. Petersburg, Florida, where he and his wife, a cocaine addict and sometime prostitute, compiled a further criminal record. In July 1994, Slatten pleaded no contest to 11 counts of petty and grand theft for a series of thefts of pay phones from laundries, post offices, and convenience stores. He would break open the phones to get the change for his wife's cocaine habit. On probation six months later, the apartment manager at the complex where Slatten was living evicted him, and Slatten became enraged. Rather than retaliate against the manager, however, he decided to go after the manager's parents. On 25 February 1995, Slatten made a pipe bomb in his living room and convinced a friend to detonate it against the front door of the manager's parents' home. The explosion damaged the house but failed to injure the sleeping inhabitants. Slatten pleaded guilty to seven counts that included making, possessing, and conspiring to use a "weapon of mass destruction." At the age of 31, in August 1996 he was sentenced to another 24 years in prison.

U.P.I.   19 Apr 1984, "U.S. Air Force Sergeant Charged with Spying"
Tampa [Florida] Tribune   14 Apr 1995, "Police: Angry Tenant Sought Revenge with Bomb"
St. Petersburg Times   5 Jul 1995, "Teenager Gets Year in Jail in DUI-Manslaughter Case"
St. Petersburg Times   16 Aug 1996, "Revenge Bomber Gets a 24-year Sentence"

SLAVENS, BRIAN EVERETT, Marine Corps PFC, reportedly deserted his sentry post at the Marine's Modified Advanced Undersea Weapons Command, Adak, Alaska. He advised his sister that he did not intend to return to the Marine Corps and that he had visited the Soviet Embassy in Washington, DC, during late August/early September 1982. Slavens's father alerted the Marine Corps of his son's intent to desert, and abruptly Slavens was arrested by Naval Investigative Service special agents on 4 September 1982. During interrogation, Slavens admitted entering the Soviet Embassy in Washington, DC, and offering to provide information concerning the military installation where he worked in Adak. Slavens denied transferring any classified material to the Soviets, but explained that his intent was to sell US military information for $500 to $1,000. According to Slavens, he was actually inside the Soviet Embassy less than 30 minutes, during which time he was asked to provide an autobiographical sketch and to reconsider his actions. Slavens subsequently requested legal counsel, and his lawyer later agreed for Slavens to undergo a polygraph examination. Slavens was administered a polygraph exam on 5 September 1982, the results of which indicated that he did not disclose any classified information to the Soviets. On 24 November 1982, Slavens pleaded guilty to a charge of attempted espionage at a general court-martial held at Marine Corps Base, Camp Lejeune, North Carolina. He was sentenced to two years' confinement and forfeiture of all pay and allowances, and given a dishonorable discharge.

Naval Investigative Service Command, *Espionage*, 1989

SMITH, JAMES J., an FBI agent, and **KATRINA M. LEUNG**, a Chinese-American business woman and Los Angeles socialite, were both arrested 9 April 2003 for illegal activities involving US classified information. Smith, 59, was charged with gross negligence in allowing Leung access to classified material, and Leung, 49, with illegally obtaining secret documents that would be an advantage to China. Leung was one of the FBI's most highly paid assets; she was paid $1.6 million for working as an informant from the early 1980s until 2002. However, it was alleged that for at least 10 years Leung was also spying for the People's Republic of China (PRC) against the US. Moreover, she had for 20 years been involved in an intimate relationship with Smith, her FBI handler. Smith routinely debriefed Leung and on occasion took classified documents to her home and left them unattended. Leung surreptitiously photocopied some of them; these same copies were later recovered from her home by the FBI. In 1991

Smith learned from the FBI that Leung was suspected of providing classified information to PRC intelligence services without authorization from the FBI, yet he continued to vouch for her and allow her access to classified materials. On her arrest, Leung was not charged by federal prosecutors with espionage (because the government could not prove she passed information to China) but with illegally copying classified documents she took from Smith's briefcase. In May 2004 Smith plea-bargained, pleading guilty only to lying about the long-time sexual affair. Four additional felony charges were dropped, which spared him from prison, but he was also barred from contact with Leung's defense lawyers because of concerns over classified information being revealed in open court. In addition, he agreed to cooperate with the government in its investigation of Leung. However, in January 2005 the case against Leung was thrown out on the grounds that she would not be able to get a fair trial without access to Smith. She ultimately pleaded guilty to two minor charges: lying to the FBI and failing to report taxable income. She spent three months in jail and 18 months in home detention, served three years' probation and 100 hours of community service, and paid a $10,000 fine. At the same time that Leung had her affair with Smith, she was also having a sexual relationship with another FBI agent, then working in San Francisco, William Cleveland Jr. He was not arrested or charged alongside Smith and Leung, but two days after Leung's arrest in 2003, he resigned his security job at the Lawrence Livermore National Laboratory.

Washington Post	13 May 2004, "Ex-Handler of Alleged FBI Spy Cuts Deal"
New York Times	7 Jan 2005, "All Charges are Dismissed in Spy Case Tied to F.B.I."
Latimes.com	5 Feb 2005, "Judge Urged to Reverse Decision Ending FBI Espionage Case"
Washington Post	25 May 2006, "FBI Officials are Faulted in Chinese Spying Case"

SMITH, RICHARD CRAIG, former Army counterintelligence agent, was arrested on 4 April 1984 and indicted for selling information to Soviet agents regarding the identities of six double-agents in the US. Having failed in business after leaving government service and faced with severe financial difficulties, Smith reportedly met on three occasions with KGB officers in Tokyo and received $11,000 for classified information. Smith himself initiated contact with the FBI in the summer of 1983, claiming he had "conned" the Soviets out of $11,000. Later, Smith claimed that he had been working under the direction of CIA operatives in Honolulu. After months of pre-trial litigation over the admissibility of evidence, Smith was acquitted by a Federal jury on 11 April 1986.

Washington Post	9 Apr 1984, "Unlikely Character for a Spy Story"
Washington Post	11 Apr 1984, "Spy-Case Suspect....."
Washington Post	13 Apr 1986, "Smith Celebrates His Freedom"

SMITH, TIMOTHY STEVEN, 37, was a civilian serving as an ordinary seaman on the *USS Kilauea*, an ammunition and supply vessel attached to the Pacific Fleet. On 1 April 2000, while the ship was moored at the Bremerton Naval Station in Bremerton, Washington, Smith was surprised by an officer when removing computer disks from a desk drawer. After a scuffle, Smith was subdued and 17 disks were retrieved from his clothing. A search of his quarters found five stolen documents marked Confidential, including one describing the transfer of ammunition and handling of torpedoes on US Navy vessels. Charged initially in US District Court in Tacoma, Washington, with two counts of espionage and two counts of theft and resisting arrest, investigation showed that Smith needed mental treatment and had a severe alcohol problem. He told FBI agents that he "wanted to get back at the crew" for their mistreatment of him and that, in order to get revenge, he had tried to steal "valuable classified materials" because "if I got something valuable, then I could turn my life around." To sell his cache, he thought he might "go online and solicit buyers from terrorist groups." Smith pleaded guilty after prosecutors dropped espionage charges. In a plea agreement reached in August 2000, he pled guilty to one count of stealing government property and one count of assaulting an officer. He was sentenced in December 2000 to 260 days' confinement (to include time served) and was released on 22 December 2000.

Seattle Post-Intelligencer   14 Apr 2000, "Seaman Admits Stealing Defense Secrets, FBI Says"
National Counter-   News and Developments, Vol. 1, March 2001
   intelligence Executive

SOMBOLAY, ALBERT T., a specialist 4th class with the Army artillery, pleaded guilty in July 1991 to espionage and aiding the enemy. He was tried by military judge in Baumholder, Germany, and sentenced to confinement at hard labor for 34 years, reduction to E-1, forfeiture of all pay and allowances, and dishonorable discharge. Sombolay was born in Zaire, Africa. He became a US citizen in 1978 and entered the Army in 1985 as a cannon crewman. In December 1990, assigned to the 8th Infantry Division in Baumholder, Germany, he contacted the Iraqi and Jordanian embassies to volunteer his services in support of the "Arab cause." To the Jordanian Embassy in Brussels he passed information on US troop readiness and promised more information to include videotapes of US equipment and positions in Saudi Arabia. He told the Jordanians that he would be deployed to Saudi Arabia and could provide them useful information. To the Iraqi Embassy in Bonn, Germany, he offered the same services, but the embassy did not respond. On 29 December, Sombolay's unit was deployed to Saudi Arabia, as part of Desert Shield, without him. Still in Germany, Sombolay continued to contact the Iraqis and provided a Jordanian representative several items of chemical warfare equipment (chemical suit, boots, gloves, and decontamination gear). His activity was discovered by US Army military intelligence. After Sombolay's arrest in March 1991, he admitted to providing Desert Shield deployment information, military identification cards, and chemical protection equipment to Jordanian officials. His motivation was money.

Huntsville Times   4 Dec 1991, "Army Spy Sentenced to 34 Years"
Cincinnati Post   7 Dec 1991, "Anatomy of a Spy"

SOUTHER, GLENN MICHAEL. On 11 July 1988, Soviet newspaper *Izvestia* announced that Souther, a former navy photographic specialist who disappeared in May 1986, had been granted political asylum in the Soviet Union. Just before his disappearance, Souther, a recent graduate with a major in Russian Studies from Old Dominion University, was questioned by FBI counterintelligence agents. According to one source, investigators were acting "on more than suspicions, but didn't catch him in the act of espionage, and thus couldn't hold Souther at the time he was questioned." While attending college, Souther had been assigned as an active reservist to the Navy Intelligence Center in Norfolk where he had access to classified information. Souther's sudden disappearance was of considerable concern to FBI and Navy officials since the former Navy enlisted man had held special security clearances while on active duty with the Sixth Fleet in the early 1980s. During that time he had access to highly classified photo-intelligence materials. Souther joined the Navy in 1975 and left active duty in 1982 with the position of photographers mate. According to the Soviets, the former Navy specialist had asked for asylum because "he had to hide from the US special services which were pursuing him groundlessly." Described as a bright but undisciplined young man by former teachers and acquaintances, Souther reportedly had wanted to become a US Naval officer, but had been turned down as a Navy officer candidate. On 22 June 1989, at the age of 32, he reportedly committed suicide by asphyxiation after shutting himself in his garage and starting his car. Russian newspapers suggested he had been disappointed by aspects of Soviet life after defecting in 1986 and was prone to depression.

Washington Post   18 Jul 1988, "Ex-Sailor Defects to Soviets"

SPADE, HENRY OTTO, a former Navy radio operator, was arrested in Mountain Home, Arkansas, on 17 November 1988 for the unauthorized possession of two Top Secret documents. One of the documents was a cryptographic key card. Spade, who was discharged from the Navy in April 1988, stole the items while on active duty, but had reportedly made no attempt to sell them to any person or foreign government. While in the Navy, Spade served aboard the USS *Midway* and the USS *Bristol County*. Charged with one count of espionage, Spade pleaded innocent and was released on $25,000 bond. Spade faced up to 10 years in prison and a $250,000 fine when convicted, but on 14 March 1989 was sentenced to three months' probation.

Washington Post   18 Nov 1988, "Ex-Sailor Charged in Secrets Case"

STAND, KURT ALAN, a regional labor union representative along with his wife, **THERESE MARIE SQUILLACOTE**, a former senior staff lawyer in the Office of the Deputy Under Secretary of Defense, and friend **JAMES MICHAEL CLARK**, a private investigator, were arrested 4 Oct 1997 on charges of spying for East Germany and Russia. Stand reportedly began his spying activities in 1972 after being recruited by East Germany to cultivate other spies in the Washington, DC, area. He was introduced to East German intelligence officers (the Stasi) through his father, Maxmillian Stand, a chemical engineer who fled Nazi Germany in the 1930s. Clark, Squillacote, and Stand attended the University of Wisconsin in the 1970s where they were affiliated with leftist groups, specifically the Progressive Student Forum and the Young Workers Liberation League, the youth arm of the Communist Party USA. Stand recruited Clark in 1976 and Squillacote about the time the couple was married in 1980. Before obtaining a position at the Pentagon, Therese Squillacote was employed by the National Labor Relations Board and, later, the House Armed Services Committee. She sent numerous photographs to her German handlers. Squillacote reportedly told an undercover FBI agent that she turned to spying to support the progressive antiimperialist movement. She first came to the attention of the FBI in 1995 when she offered to be a spy in a letter to a South African government official who was a leader of his country's Communist Party. Stand and Squillacote frequently traveled to Mexico, Germany, and Canada during which time Stand would meet with their East German handlers. When the two Germanys united in 1990, Stand's controllers tried to recruit him to spy for the Soviet Union and then for the Russian Federation. Although he never gained access to classified material, his role in the operation was to recruit agents and to provide information about the nongovernmental groups with which he worked. Stand allegedly received $24,650 for his recruiting and coordinating efforts. On 23 Oct 1998, he and Squillacote were convicted of conspiracy to commit espionage, attempted espionage, and illegally obtaining national defense documents. On 22 January 1999, a US District Judge sentenced Squillacote to 21 years and 10 months in prison and Stand to a sentence of 17 years and six months. [See also the case summary for James Michael Clark.]

New York Times   7 Oct 1997, "Three Onetime Radicals Held in Spy Case"
Washington Post   2 Nov 1997, "Cloak and Blabber; A Story of Espionage and Very Loose Lips"
Washington Post   24 Oct 1998, "Jury Rejects Entrapment Defense, Convicts DC Couple of Spying"

TOBIAS, MICHAEL TIMOTHY, Navy Petty Officer 3rd Class, along with his nephew, **FRANCIS X. PIZZO**, were arrested on 13 August 1985 and charged with stealing Top Secret cryptographic key cards from the USS *Peoria*, berthed at San Diego. The pair were also accused of attempting to sell the material to representatives of the Soviet Union for $100,000. Tobias and Pizzo drove to the Soviet Consulate in San Francisco, but arrived during the early morning before regular business hours. Having failed in their initial attempt to contact a "foreign power," and obviously having second thoughts about committing espionage, the pair drove back to San Diego and called the US Secret Service offering to sell the cards back to the government for amnesty and money by claiming that they were prepared to sell the key material to the Soviets. Several calls were placed to the Secret Service by Pizzo, one of which was traced by the FBI. Also arrested in connection with the case were Tobias's brother, **BRUCE TOBIAS**, and **DALE IRENE** of San Diego. According to government prosecutors, Tobias took the classified cards from the ship instead of shredding them, as was his assignment with the intention of selling them. Pizzo pleaded guilty to five Federal charges and on 7 October was sentenced to 10 years in prison. Bruce Tobias and Dale Irene pleaded guilty to two counts of receiving stolen property. During the four-day trial of Michael Tobias, an NSA official testified that the cards would have provided sensitive information about the location and movement of US and foreign vessels. Two of the 12 pilfered cards have not been recovered. On 14 August Michael Tobias was found guilty of four counts of conspiracy and three counts of theft of government property. The US Attorney stated that Tobias had attempted to leave the country and that he and Pizzo had been seen near the Soviet Consulate in San Francisco before their arrests. On 12 November 1995, Michael Tobias was sentenced to 20 years' imprisonment; in January 1996, Bruce Tobias was sentenced to the prison time he served up to that date (159 days), and Dale Irene was sentenced to a two-year confinement.

New York Times   15 Aug 1985, "Sailor is Guilty of Conspiring to Sell Secret Data from Ship"
New York Times   13 Nov 1985, "Sailor Sentenced to 20 Years for Trying to Sell 11 Navy Codes"
Naval Investigative Service Command, Espionage, 1989

TROFIMOFF, GEORGE, retired US Army Reserve colonel, 73, was arrested on 14 June 2000 in Tampa, Florida, and charged with spying for Russia for 25 years. His arrest concluded a seven-year investigation by the FBI and German authorities. According to the FBI, Trofimoff provided classified information to the Russians while employed in a civilian job in Nuremburg, Germany, from 1959 to 1994, following his military retirement. He allegedly was paid $250,000 for documents provided to KGB, and later, to SVR agents. According the indictment, Trofimoff, who was raised in Germany by Russian émigré parents, was recruited by **IGOR SUSEMIHL**, a Russian Orthodox priest and Trofimoff's boyhood friend. Trofimoff enlisted in the US Army in 1948 after his family moved to the US, and he became a US citizen in 1951. He received a commission in the Army Reserve in 1953 and retired with the rank of colonel in 1987. During his military and civilian careers he held Secret or Top Secret security clearances, and in his civilian position, with the Army 66th Military Intelligence Group, he had access to a wide variety of classified materials including US intelligence needs and objectives. In or about 1969, Trofimoff was recruited into the service of the KGB by Susemihl, who at the time served as archbishop of Austria. Susemihl died in 1999. Trofimoff allegedly removed classified documents from the US Army Interrogation Center in Munich, photographed and returned the originals, and then passed the film to Susemihl or KGB agents during several meetings in Austria or southern Germany. It is believed that he turned over more than 50,000 pages of classified documents. Trofimoff and Susemihl had been arrested by German authorities for suspected espionage in 1994, but the case was dropped because the statute of limitations had expired. The investigation, however, was continued by US officials. In late 2000, Trofimoff, who had since retired to Florida, was approached by an FBI agent posing as a Russian officer who offered a "special payment" for additional information. Before his arrest at a Tampa hotel, Trofimoff met with undercover FBI agents several times and was videotaped fully admitting his past involvement in espionage. However, the retired Army employee pleaded not guilty on 26 June, 2001, claiming that he was a loyal American who was just trying to collect some money to cover his debts. Trofimoff, the highest ranking US officer ever accused of spying, was convicted in June for his role in the 25-year espionage conspiracy after a four-week trial. He was sentenced to life imprisonment on 27 September 2001.

Orlando Sentinel   15 Jun 2000, "Viera Retiree is Accused of Espionage"
Stars and Stripes   1 Jul 2000, "Trofimoff Denies He Spied for Soviets"
Washington Post   6 Jun 2001, "Espionage Trial Begins for Retired Army Colonel"

| *Miami Herald* | 25 Jun 2001, "Historic Spy Trial in Tampa Nears End" |
| *New York Times* | 27 Jun 2001, "Retired Army Employee is Found Guilty of Spying" |

TSOU, DOUGLAS, a Chinese-born former FBI employee, was indicted in 1988 on one count of espionage following his admission that in 1986 he had written a letter to a representative of the government of Taiwan in which he revealed the identity of an intelligence officer of the People's Republic of China. According to testimony at the trial (which was delayed until October 1991), the unidentified agent operating in Taiwan had unsuccessfully approached the FBI with an offer to work as a double agent. Although the information Tsou passed to a Taiwanese representative in Houston was classified as Secret, Tsou claimed that he considered the information to be declassified since the offer was not accepted. Motivation for his acts of espionage was likely loyalty to government of Taiwan. Tsou fled to Taiwan when the communists rose to power on the mainland in 1949 and moved to the US 20 years later where he became a naturalized citizen. He worked for the FBI from 1980 to 1986, first in San Francisco and later in Houston. On 4 October 1991, Tsou was found guilty as charged. However, prosecutors claimed that this represented only the tip of the iceberg of what Tsou gave to Taiwanese officials during his six years with the FBI. On 2 January 1992, Tsou was sentenced to a 10-year Federal prison term.

| *Houston Chronicle* | 22 Jan 1992, "Ex-FBI Translator Sentenced for Passing Secrets to Taiwan" |

TUMANOVA, SVETLANA, a naturalized US citizen born in Estonia, worked as a secretary at the US Army Foreign Language Training Center in Munich. She married a Soviet émigré and her parents continued to live in the Soviet Union. In 1978 she was recruited by the Soviet foreign intelligence service to provide information through coercion based on threats against her parents. Arrested in 1987 by West German police, she was convicted of providing biographical information on personnel at the Language Center for nine years. She was sentenced to five years' probation.

WALKER, ARTHUR JAMES, a retired Navy Lieutenant Commander, was arrested on 29 May 1985 for providing classified material to his brother in 1981 and 1982. Arthur Walker was employed with a defense contractor in Chesapeake, Virginia, where he reportedly sought work in early 1980 at the urging of his brother, John A. Walker, to gain access to classified documents. During the period of his employment, Arthur Walker provided his brother with several Confidential documents that related to ship construction and design. These were photocopied and returned to the firm's classified container. In all Arthur Walker received $12,000 for his collaboration, much of which he returned to his brother to repay a debt. His motive for participating in John Walker's scheme was both for money and to help this brother. On 9 August 1985, he was found guilty of seven counts of espionage by a US District Court judge. On 12 November, Arthur Walker was sentenced to life imprisonment and fined $250,000. At the time of sentencing it was revealed that polygraph tests indicated Walker may have been involved in espionage while on active duty with the Navy.

Washington Post	7 Aug 1985, "Two Portraits of Arthur Walker: Subversive Plotter"
Washington Post	10 Aug 1985, "Walker Guilty of Espionage on 7 Counts"
Time Magazine	19 Aug 1985, "A Spy Ring Goes to Court"
New York Times	13 Nov 1985, "Arthur Walker Sentenced to Life; Wider Spying Role"

WALKER, JOHN ANTHONY, and his son, **MICHAEL LANCE WALKER**, were indicted 28 May 1985 by a Federal grand jury in Baltimore on six counts of espionage. The elder Walker, a retired Navy warrant officer who had held a Top Secret crypto clearance, was charged with having sold classified material to Soviet agents for the past 18 years. During his military career, Walker made some investments in which he lost money. To make up for his losses, in late 1968 at the age of 30, Walker went to the Soviet Embassy in Washington, DC, and offered his services for purposes of espionage. He compromised key cards used for enciphering messages and also provided information on the encryption devices themselves. At least a million classified messages of the military services and US intelligence agencies were compromised. A Soviet defector said the KGB considered this the most important operation in its history. Michael Walker, a petty officer assigned to the USS *Nimitz*, was accused of providing classified Navy documents to his father for sale to the Soviets. Fifteen pounds of classified material were in his possession at the time of arrest on the *Nimitz*. John Walker's arrest resulted from a tip to the FBI from his former wife. He was apprehended at a Maryland motel after depositing a number of documents at a roadside drop. Soviet Embassy official, Alexei Tkachenko, who was spotted in the area, returned to Moscow within days of Walker's arrest. It is also alleged that John Walker recruited his brother, **ARTHUR JAMES WALKER**, and former Navy friend, **JERRY ALFRED WHITWORTH**, as sources of classified information for Soviet intelligence (see separate summaries for these cases). On 28 October, both John and Michael Walker pleaded guilty to espionage charges under a plea agreement by which the senior Walker agreed to testify in the trial of Jerry Whitworth and to provide full information on what was given to the Soviets in exchange for a lesser sentence for his son. On 6 November 1986, John Walker was sentenced to two life terms plus 10 years to be served concurrently. Michael was sentenced to 25 years. A Federal grand jury has been convened to pursue some of the unresolved questions including the location of up to $1 million possibly hidden by John Walker, and the involvement of minor players in the espionage ring.

New York Times   21 May 1985, "Ex-Navy Officer Is Charged With Espionage"
Washington Post   22 May 1985, "Spy Suspect's Son Queried"
Washington Post   16 Aug 1985, "Lawyers Admit Walker Left Bag"
Washington Post   29 Oct 1985, "2 Walkers Plead Guilty to Spying"
Washington Post   7 Nov 1986, "Walker Gets Life Term; Judge to Oppose Parole"
Naval Investigative Service Command, *Espionage*, 1989

WARREN, KELLY THERESE, a former US Army clerk, was arrested 10 June 1997 and named in a three-count indictment alleging her involvement in the passing of sensitive information to Hungary and Czechoslovakia in the mid-80's, as a part of the **CLYDE LEE CONRAD** spy ring. Warren was charged with conspiracy to aid a foreign government and gathering or delivering classified national defense information. From 1986 to 1988 she had been assigned as an administrative assistant in the section that handled war plans for the Army's 8th Infantry Division headquarters in Bad Kreuznach, Germany. In 1987 she was recruited into the Conrad ring by then-coworker **RODERICK JAMES RAMSAY**. Among documents Warren gave to Conrad to pass to Hungarian and Czech agents were secret US and NATO plans for the defense of Western Europe in the event of a Soviet bloc attack. The indictment said that Warren met with Conrad on base, at a bowling alley and in a church in Bad Kreuznach, to trade cash for secrets. She earned only $7,000 for her efforts with which she claimed to have paid off debts, money being her motive. Federal agents had suspected her involvement for almost 10 years. According to a plea agreement, Warren pled guilty to one count of conspiracy to commit espionage on 6 November 1998 and on 12 February she was sentenced to 25 years in prison. Warren is the seventh US service member to be charged with taking part in the Conrad spy ring since 1988.

Florida Times-Union   11 Jun 1997, "Former Soldier Arrested; Warner Robins Woman Charged in
                            Espionage Case"
Raleigh News and Observer 29 Jul 1997, "Federal Agents Still Tracking Members of '80s Army Spy Ring"

WEINMANN, ARIEL JONATHAN, 22 at the time of his sentencing, joined the Navy in 2003, having recently graduated from high school in Salem, Oregon. That same year he had met a girl with whom he fell in love. However, her anti-war parents did not approve of her dating a sailor. In the Navy he became a fire control technician, which involved operating and maintaining submarine weapons systems. Weinmann deployed to the submarine, *Albuquerque*. He quickly became unhappy with life on the sub, describing it as "morally corrupt." After his tour of duty he returned home to be informed by his girlfriend that her parents did not approve of the relationship and that she was being sent to college in Switzerland. The next day he told her that if he did not hear from her by his October birthday, he would move on with his life. Following her departure, Weinmann moved to Austria to be near her. Before he left for Austria, he downloaded classified information from the ship's database that he hoped would gain him asylum in Austria. These documents included biographical information on 29 prominent Austrians that the US government had compiled and also technical manuals on the Tomahawk cruise missile system. With his $7,000 savings, he arrived in Vienna at the beginning of July 2005. The October deadline passed with no word from the girlfriend, and that same month he entered the Russian Embassy in Vienna, handing the official a binder full of classified documents on the Tomahawk system. He never heard back from the official. When he realized that he had given away his only leverage, Weinmann decided to go to Russia to seek asylum there. However, that meant returning to the US first. On 26 March 2006, he flew from Mexico City to Dallas Fort Worth where he was arrested by US Customs agents because his name appeared on a deserter watch list. However, apparently he had not given away all his classified documents; some were found in his backpack, which led to the espionage charges. Weinmann pleaded guilty at court-martial to espionage, desertion, theft, and destruction of military property. He was sentenced 10 December 2006 to 25 years in prison, a dishonorable discharge, a reduction in rank, and forfeiture of all pay and allowances. A plea agreement limited his prison sentence to 12 years and he will be eligible for parole after four.

| *Virginian-Pilot* | 10 Dec 2006, "Why a Patriotic Teen Joined the Navy and Then Turned to Espionage" |
| *StatesmanJournal.com (Salem, OR)* | 11 Dec 2006, "Jilted Love, Not Political Intrigue, Drove a Salem Man to Espionage" |

WHITWORTH, JERRY ALFRED, collaborator with **JOHN A. WALKER**, surrendered to FBI agents on 3 June 1985 following the issue of a complaint charging him with conspiracy to commit espionage. Whitworth, a retired Naval communications specialist who had held a Top Secret clearance, is alleged to have received $332,000 through Walker for highly classified information related to Naval communications between 1975 and 1982. FBI sources state that Whitworth had attempted to arrange a meeting with them in 1984 in order to bargain for immunity from prosecution. According to one news item, of all the alleged participants in the Walker spy ring the damage attributed to Whitworth is thought to be the worst since he is reported to have provided the Soviets with key lists that would have enabled them to decode US Naval communications, and classified information about the design of cryptographic equipment. Whitworth pleaded innocent to a 13-count indictment, but during his subsequent trial, defense lawyers admitted that he had passed classified materials to John Walker. However, the argument that he did not know these highly classified cryptographic materials were ending up in Soviet hands was not accepted by the Federal jury. Following a highly publicized three-month trial, Whitworth was convicted on 12 counts of espionage and tax evasion. The former communications specialist received a sentence of 365 years and a fine of $410,000 on 28 August 1986.

Washington Post	4 Jun 1985, "4th Arrested in Spy Case"
Washington Post	8 Jun 1985, "Agent Believes Sailor Said He Passed Data"
Washington Post	14 Jun 1985, "Accused Spy 'A Quiet Man'"

WILMOTH, JAMES R., US Navy airman recruit, was a food service worker aboard the carrier USS *Midway*. He was arrested by Naval Investigative Service agents in Yokosuka in July 1989 for attempting to sell classified information to a Soviet agent in Japan, where the *Midway* is based. He was tried and convicted at a general military court-martial 24 September 1989. In addition to attempted espionage, Wilmoth was convicted of failure to report a contact with a citizen of the Soviet Union, conspiracy to unlawfully transfer classified material, and possession, use and distribution of hashish. He was sentenced to 35 years at hard labor; however, since he cooperated in the investigation, his sentence was reduced to 15 years. He also received a dishonorable discharge, and was ordered to forfeit all his pay. He had been in the Navy for over two years and had a history of disciplinary problems including unauthorized leave of absence. Wilmoth did not have a security clearance. Classified information was procured by Petty Officer Third Class **RUSSELL PAUL BROWN** also stationed aboard the *Midway*. Brown held a Secret security clearance and took classified documents obtained from the burn bag in the electronic warfare center of the *Midway*. He passed the documents to Wilmoth, who planned to exchange the documents for cash in an arrangement with a KGB operative in Japan. Brown was convicted in October 1989 of conspiracy to commit espionage and lying to Navy investigators. A military judge sentenced him to 10 years in prison, a dishonorable discharge, reduction in rank from E-3 to E-1, and forfeiture of all pay and allowances. Motivation for the attempted sale to the Soviets was money.

Los Angeles Times	5 Oct 1989, "Sailor Sentenced to 35 Years After Attempted Espionage"
Washington Times	5 Oct 1989, "Navy Convicts Spy, Stalks Another"
Washington Times	25 Oct 1989, "2nd Midway Sailor Gets Jail Term for Spying"

WISPELAERE, JEAN-PHILIPPE, 28, while employed by the Australian Defense Intelligence Organization as an analyst, in 1999 downloaded hundreds of sensitive classified US military documents to his computer and removed the files from his office. He was cleared for access to Top Secret US information. These documents, reported to be related to US satellite reconnaissance, were provided to Australia under a defense sharing agreement. On 18 January, six days after his unexpected resignation from the Australian intelligence agency, Wispelaere, posing as a Canadian official, walked into the embassy of Singapore in Bangkok and offered to sell the classified documents. He left a sample classified document and his email address. The US was alerted about the contact and set up a sting operation. At a later meeting at a Bangkok hotel with undercover FBI agents, Wispelaere turned over 713 classified US documents maps and photos for $70,000 and subsequently mailed more than 200 items to a post office box in Virginia set up by the FBI for another $50,000. At one point, Wispelaere told the agent that he was in "dire financial need" and that this "involved females." He was lured to Virginia to accept another payment, and on 15 May 1999 was arrested at Dulles International Airport upon his arrival from London. He initially pleaded not guilty, but later entered into a plea agreement by which he was required to reveal all of his illegal activities. Sentencing was delayed when Wispelaere was diagnosed with schizophrenia, and for a time he was declared unfit to stand trial. On June 9, 2001, he was sentenced to 15 years in prison after the government announced that he had lived up to the terms of the plea agreement.

Los Angeles Times	18 May 1999, "Internet-savvy Australian Charged in Espionage Case"
Calgary Herald	21 May 1999, "Canadian Spy Was 'a Bit of a Bumbler'"
Washington Post	9 Jun 2001, "15-year Term in Espionage Case: Australian Stole U.S. Documents, Tried to Sell Them"

WOLD, HANS PALMER was an Intelligence Specialist Third Class assigned to the USS *Ranger* when he asked for and was given leave from 13 June through 2 July 1983. The leave was granted with the understanding that Wold would stay in the local San Diego area, but around 2 July Wold's command received a message from the American Red Cross, Subic Bay, Philippines, in which Wold requested an extension of leave. Wold's request was granted for five additional days of leave. However, he failed to report for duty on 7 July and was listed as an unauthorized absentee. Wold's command then asked the Naval Investigative Service to locate him and turn him over to US Naval Forces in the Philippines at Subic Bay for appropriate debriefing. On 19 July 1983 Wold was picked up by NIS special agents at his fiancée's residence in Olongapo City, in the Philippines, for being absent without leave. During Wold's apprehension, an undeveloped roll of film was seized. During his debriefing Wold told an intelligence specialist that the roll of film had photographs from a Top Secret publication. Wold admitted he had covertly photographed the publication, "Navy Application of National Reconnaissance Systems (U)," while onboard the USS *Ranger* during June 1983, and intended to contact the Soviets. While he never did contact the Soviets, his motivation was to sell the materials for money. On 5 October 1983, Wold pleaded guilty at a general court-martial to unauthorized absence, using marijuana onboard the USS *Ranger*, false swearing, and "making photographs with intent or reason to believe information was to be used to the injury of the US or the advantage of a foreign nation." Wold was sentenced to four years at hard labor, a dishonorable discharge, forfeiture of all pay and allowances, and reduction in rate to E-1.

Naval Investigative Service Command, *Espionage*, 1989

WOLF, RONALD CRAIG, a former pilot in the Air Force from 1974 to 1981, was arrested 5 May 1989 in Dallas, Texas, for selling classified information to an FBI undercover officer posing as a Soviet agent. During his career in the Air Force, Wolf was trained as a Russian voice-processing specialist and flew intelligence missions on reconnaissance aircraft in the Far East. He held a Top Secret clearance. Discharged from the military in 1981 because of his unsuitability for service "due to financial irresponsibility," he worked as an automobile salesman for a while, but was unemployed at the time of his arrest. The FBI's investigation began in March 1989, when information was obtained indicating Wolf's desire to sell sensitive information to the Soviet Union. Wolf talked with FBI undercover agent "Sergei Kitin" on a number of occasions thinking he was a representative of the Soviet Union assigned to the Soviet Embassy. During these conversations Wolf talked about his military experience and his desire to defect and provide Air Force secrets "for monetary gain and to get revenge for his treatment by the United States government." He was directed to mail letters to a post office box in Maryland detailing the type of information he was capable of providing. Wolf passed along classified documents concerning Top Secret signals intelligence. The FBI says they are "confident there was no exchange of information (with foreign agents) in this case." On 28 February 1990, Wolf pleaded guilty in Federal court. In return for his guilty plea, the government reduced the severity of the charges from life imprisonment to up to 10 years in prison. In June, Wolf was sentenced to 10 years without parole.

Dallas Times Herald	1 Mar 90, "Ex-Air Force Pilot Pleads Guilty to Espionage"
Washington Post	16 Jun 90, "Ex-Airman Get 10 Years"

WOLFF, JAY CLYDE, 24-year-old auto painter and former Navy enlisted man, was arrested on 17 December 1984 in Gallup, New Mexico, for offering to sell classified documents dealing with US weapons systems aboard a US Navy vessel. Wolff, who was discharged from the Navy in 1983, met with an undercover agent and offered to sell classified material for $5,000 to $6,000. According to the FBI, a tip led to the meeting with Wolff at a convenience store where he was apprehended. Wolff pleaded guilty to one count of attempting to sell classified documents and on 28 June 1985 the former service member was sentenced to five years in prison.

YAI, JOHN JOUNGWOONG, a sandwich shop owner from Santa Monica, California, was arrested 4 February 2003 for failing to register as an agent of North Korea, failing to report bringing more than

$10,000 cash into the country, and for making false statements to US Customs inspectors. Yai, 59, who came to the US from Seoul, Korea, in 1975 and became naturalized in 1981, was accused of operating within the US at the direction of North Korean intelligence. Between December 1997 and April 2000, he was paid for his services to the North Korean government that had tasked him to obtain classified information and identify and recruit other agents. Yai was not charged with espionage because the FBI could not prove that he had been successful in collecting and passing along classified information to North Korea. He did not speak English well and did not have a job relating to the government or know anyone who did. Yet he confessed to having received over time some $40,000 from the North Koreans for passing along what amounted to publicly available documents. And he did try to recruit agents in the US. He communicated with North Korean agents through coded faxes and email messages and through meetings overseas; he traveled to North Korea, China, Austria and the Czech Republic to meet North Korean security officials. Yai had been under investigation by FBI Counterintelligence for seven years. The investigation involved surveillance, FISA-authorized secret searches, wiretaps and other high-tech electronic monitoring. On 15 November 2004 Yai was sentenced to two years in prison and was ordered to pay a $20,000 fine. His wife, who accompanied him on some trips, was sentenced to one year probation and a $500 fine.

US Department of Justice   5 Feb 2003, "Santa Monica Man Arrested for
    Field News Press Release   Failing to Register as an Agent of a Foreign Government"
Los Angeles Times   6 Feb 2003, "FBI Watched Spy Suspect for 7 Years"
Telegraph (UK)   16 Feb 2003, "Blunders of the Snack Shop 'Spy'
San Jose Mercury News   26 Apr 2003, "Spy Case Worries Korean Emigres"

ZAKHAROV, GENNADIY F., Soviet physicist employed at the United Nations Secretariat, was arrested on 23 August 1986 on a Queens, New York, subway platform as he gave $1,000 to an employee of a US defense contractor for three classified documents. Zakharov, who did not have diplomatic immunity, had attempted to recruit the employee over a period of three years. At the time of Zakharov's first approach, the individual, a Guyanese national and resident alien of the US, was in his junior year at Queens College, New York. Zakharov met with the student on numerous occasions and paid several thousand dollars for a wide range of technical but unclassified information about robotics, computers, and artificial intelligence. At the time of Zakharov's first approach in April 1983, the recruitment target, identified only by the code name "Birg," informed the FBI and agreed to work under FBI control in order to apprehend the Soviet agent. Following his graduation in 1985, Birg obtained a position with a high-technology firm. Under FBI direction, he agreed to sign a 10-year written contract with Zakharov to provide classified information. Money to be paid by the Soviets was to be determined by the quantity and quality of the information. On 30 September, Zakharov pleaded no contest to espionage charges and was ordered to leave the country within 24 hours. Zakharov's expulsion came less than 24 hours after the release of American correspondent, Nicholas Daniloff, who had been arrested in the Soviet Union for alleged espionage activities.

New York Times   24 Aug 1986, "A Soviet Official Assigned to U.N. is Seized as a Spy"
New York Times   25 Aug 1986, "Russian's Arrest Called Example of Spy Threat"
New York Times   26 Aug 1986, "US Investigating Further Spy Cases in New York Area"

ZEHE, ALFRED, an East German physicist and operative for East German intelligence, was arrested on 3 November 1983, the result of a successful sting operation. On 21 December 1981, Bill Tanner, a civilian engineer employed at the Naval Electronic Systems Engineering Center in Charleston, South Carolina, walked into the East German Embassy in Washington, DC, and offered to exchange classified information for money. Tanner was actually a double agent working under the control of the Naval

Investigative Service and FBI. The FBI's target was the East German intelligence service, the Ministerium fuer Staatssicherheit (MfS): how it worked and what type of information it was looking for. Zehe was Tanner's primary contact. Zehe is reported to be the first East German operative apprehended in this country. In July 1984, Zehe was freed on $500,000 bail to await trial. He subsequently pleaded guilty and was sentenced on 4 April to eight years' imprisonment with a fine of $5,000. In June 1985, Zehe was traded with three other Eastern Bloc agents for 25 persons who had "been helpful" to the United States.

New York Times   4 Nov 1983, "East German Held in Espionage Case"
New York Times   5 Nov 1983, "East German is Denied Bail"
Naval Investigative Service Command, *Espionage*, 1989